D1531274

THE LITTLE BOOK OF KNOWLEDGE:

SHARKS

Become our fan on Facebook **facebook.com/idwpublishing**
Follow us on Twitter **@idwpublishing**
Subscribe to us on YouTube **youtube.com/idwpublishing**
See what's new on Tumblr **tumblr.idwpublishing.com**
Check us out on Instagram **instagram.com/idwpublishing**

ISBN: 978-1-68405-066-6   21 20 19 18   1 2 3 4

LITTLE BOOK OF KNOWLEDGE: SHARKS. JULY 2018. FIRST PRINTING.
© ÉDITIONS DU LOMBARD (DARGAUD-LOMBARD S.A.) 2016, by
Solé, Séret www.lelombard.com. All rights reserved. © 2018 Idea and
Design Works, LLC. The IDW logo is registered in the U.S. Patent and
Trademark Office. IDW Publishing, a division of Idea and Design Works,
LLC. Editorial offices: 2765 Truxtun Road, San Diego, CA 92106. Any
similarities to persons living or dead are purely coincidental. With the
exception of artwork used for review purposes, none of the contents
of this publication may be reprinted without the permission of Idea and
Design Works, LLC. Printed in Korea.
IDW Publishing does not read or accept unsolicited submissions of
ideas, stories, or artwork.

Greg Goldstein, President & Publisher
Robbie Robbins, EVP & Sr. Art Director
Chris Ryall, Chief Creative Officer & Editor-in-Chief
Matthew Ruzicka, CPA, Chief Financial Officer
David Hedgecock, Associate Publisher
Laurie Windrow, Senior Vice President of Sales & Marketing
Lorelei Bunjes, VP of Digital Services
Eric Moss, Sr. Director, Licensing & Business Development

Ted Adams, Founder & CEO of IDW Media Holdings

For international rights, please
contact licensing@idwpublishing.com

Created for Editions Du Lombard by David Vandermeulen and
Nathalie Van Campenhoudt.
Original layout by Elhadi Yazi, Eric Laurin, and Rebekah Paulovich.

THE LITTLE BOOK
OF KNOWLEDGE:

SHARKS

WRITTEN BY
BERNARD SÉRET

ART BY
JULIEN SOLÉ

TRANSLATION BY
EDWARD GAUVIN

EDITS BY
JUSTIN EISINGER AND ALONZO SIMON

COLLECTION DESIGN BY
RON ESTEVEZ

PUBLISHER:
GREG GOLDSTEIN

FOREWORD
BY DAVID VANDERMEULEN

BETWEEN AVERSION AND FASCINATION

According to several recent studies surveying causes of death among humans, sharks are responsible for at most a dozen deaths of swimmers and bathers. On land, the same statistics attribute almost 25,000 deadly attacks to dogs. Curiously, the manifest threat dogs pose has in no way sullied their solid reputation as man's best friend. What's more, if reports of the havoc wrought by overfishing are to be believed, humans are without a doubt the most significant predators of sharks, killing more than 73 million per year. These figures are all the more staggering in light of the fact that many species of shark, especially the largest, have no natural predators.

The paradox is almost a given: while sharks exert an undeniable fascination over humans, they nonetheless remain an almost irrational source of fear. Unfortunately, ignorance, preconception, and prejudice remain, even today, inextricable from our ideas of sharks.

THE HISTORY OF A PHOBIA IN FIVE ACTS

ACT I
THE JERSEY SHORE SHARK ATTACKS OF 1916

Quite by chance, the book you hold in your hands came out in French almost exactly a century after the advent of the first mass phobia to coalesce around sharks. Their bad reputation and the fear they provoke were born of a very specific place and time. During the first two weeks of July 1916, between Beach Haven, Spring Lake, and Matawan Creek, three New Jersey seaside resorts on the eastern seaboard of the U.S., a series of accidents was, for the first time, to give rise to an aversion to sharks. Only four swimmers were killed, but there was such a frenzy of newspaper coverage of the event that the Jersey Shore shark attacks took on an unparalleled dimension, earning a permanent place in history and people's memories.

The American press was all too happy to cover such an unusual accident—at the time, the idea that a fish might kill a man was a new one, and hard to believe. The papers blew up the event into such widespread madness that they created, spread, and maintained a state of heretofore unseen mass hysteria in a way only the media can. People got so carried away that the devastating polio epidemic raging in New York that summer, which took some thirty lives a day and had been making headlines for weeks on end, soon gave way to tragic tales of shark encounters. The authorities banned people from going into the water, whereupon people immediately deserted the beaches, causing genuine economic hardship.

We might suspect that the minute panic affects the economy, things will be taken seriously. As America was still dithering over whether to get involved in a war against the German Empire, the shark affair took on such scope that President Woodrow Wilson himself ended up convening an emergency Cabinet meeting. They evaluated the situation and launched a shark hunt, with a fat reward thrown in to boot. Hundreds of people volunteered, such that the New Jersey shark hunts of 1916 went down as the largest scale animal hunt in history. Hunters went so far as to use dynamite!

ACT II
1945: THE SURVIVORS OF THE *U.S.S. INDIANAPOLIS*

It wasn't until late in World War II that another situation, one of undeniably tragic dimensions, rekindled shark phobia. Once again, the events involved Americans, and once again, the press did their dirty work. It all started with the sinking of the *U.S.S. Indianapolis*, a heavy cruiser that had just finished delivering elements vital to the construction of the atomic bomb Little Boy. In the Philippine Sea, on the night of July 30, 1945, after leaving the naval base on Tinian in the Mariana Islands, the *Indianapolis* was torpedoed by a Japanese submarine. It was hit directly in the fuel tank, which contained 3,500 gallons of fuel. The ten-thousand ton cruiser sank in less than twelve minutes, and of the 1,196 men in its crew, 900 managed to survive the explosion by jumping into the water. The final survivors weren't fished out till August 8th, one very long week later, between the bombings of Hiroshima and Nagasaki on August 6th and 9th, respectively. Of the 900 sailors who threw themselves into the water, only 317 were saved: all exhausted, in shock, and terrorized... by sharks. Naturally, American papers had a field day with this abominable tragedy, publishing a host of sordid first-hand accounts that only reignited old fears left over from 1916. However, though it is indisputable that the massive explosion, the unusual amount of activity in the water, and blood from the wounded sailors did draw an uncommon number of sharks, estimates of the number of sailors who died from shark attacks vary, according to accounts, from 30 to 150. Many sailors simply succumbed to heat and thirst, poisoned when they couldn't keep from drinking saltwater. A good number of them fell prey to hallucinations, slipping into madness and panic attacks. At any rate, though, the damage was done. From then on, the tragedy of the *U.S.S. Indianapolis* would long remain synonymous with Japanese torpedoes, shipwreck, and heroes devoured by sharks.

ACT III
1954: COUSTEAU, THE EMBARRASSING AMBASSADOR

If demonizing sharks has primarily been an activity of the English-speaking world, France, so as not to be outdone, certainly played its part. Most of said part was in fact played by an unlikely figure: Captain Jacques Cousteau. In what has become an infamous scene from *The Silent World*[1], crewmembers from the *Calypso* wrathfully harpoon several sharks, drag them on board, and finish them off with sledgehammers while Jacques-Yves Cousteau, in voiceover, declares with timeless gravity: "All sailors hate sharks." It goes without saying that the story of the *Indianapolis* left its mark on sailors worldwide. And when Cousteau gave voice to their antipathy for sharks, he was in all likelihood merely echoing a fairly universal sentiment for the 1950s. But sixty years later, it is clear that such unconsidered reflections have no business being in a nature documentary. Today, such a clear-cut and unnuanced point of view would make audiences laugh if the hatred of sharks Cousteau finds so acceptable hadn't left an imprint on so many minds. It is unfortunate that only recently have we begun to realize the sheer extent of the harmful influence that Cousteau's words and images had on generations of children and viewers.

ACT IV
1974: PETER BENCHLEY PUTS A NAIL IN THE COFFIN

In early 1970, reporter Peter Benchley, who'd just lost his job as a speechwriter to President Johnson, got an itch to write a novel. One day in 1971, Benchley showed up at the office of Thomas Congdon, a major editor at Doubleday, carrying under one arm a draft of a horror novel strongly inspired by newspaper articles from 1916 covering the Spring Lake shark attacks. In his novel, Benchley had moved the events to the modern era and slightly further north, to the fictional seaside resort town of Amity, New York. The project interested Congdon, though writing it was a chore at first: Benchley was forced to make major revisions, as his editor found the tone too lighthearted. In the end, the hard work paid off. When it came out in February 1974, Peter Benchley's *Jaws* was an immediate success, staying on the bestseller list for 44 weeks in a row. Less than a year later, the book had been translated into several languages and sold 7.6 million copies. The phenomenon

soon d   of two producers at Universal Pictures, Richard Zanuck
and D   ） raced to buy the rights and offered Benchley a shot at
adapt   vel to the screen.

ACT V
1975: THE ULTIMATE DEMONIZATION: SPIELBERG'S TERROR MACHINE

Benchley, Carl Gottlieb, and no less than five other writers had a hand in the
screenplay for *Jaws*. Two of them, Howard Sackler and John Milius, managed to
convince a reluctant Benchley, to include the disaster of the *U.S.S. Indianapolis*[2].
The director's reins were handed over to Steven Spielberg, then a little-known
young man barely 28 years old. The shoot was plagued with setbacks. There was
a series of technical problems with the great white shark they'd built, such that
Spielberg had to leave out several key scenes. Luckily for the young director, Verna
"Mother Cutter" Fields, one of Hollywood's most famous editors, was on the job.
She was also close to Ned Tanen, then president of Universal. In promotional
interviews for the movie, Spielberg kept bringing up the ingenious and inventive
tricks Fields had taught him, sometimes going so far as to present them as his own
ideas. He came off as a humble follower of the law that Alfred Hitchcock, the
master of fear, had established: leave the horror to the audience's imagination. In
the end, the expensive shark that had cost the production so much showed up only
in a few shots. And the technical issues suddenly turned into a blessing that made
the movie even scarier. Thanks to Verna Fields'[3] gifts , Spielberg's film inspired an
unbridled terror not unlike the feeling anybody might have imagining themselves
being devoured alive by something they couldn't quite see. Having triumphed over
the difficulties of the shoot, Universal then focused all its energy on making *Jaws*
the first summer blockbuster in the history of film. Eight months before its release,
the crew invited Benchley and two of the six other writers of the screenplay to take
part in promoting the movie. The writers gave a number of interviews whose only
goal was to paint great white sharks as terrifying monsters, hungry for fresh meat
during high season at the beach. When the film was released on June 20, 1975, the
studio indulged in an ad campaign the likes of which had never before been seen
in the history of the Seventh Art. More than four hundred theaters were showing

the film. For three days straight, every radio station and TV channel across the American continent ran spots full of screams, cries, and the worst, most horrifying descriptions of great white sharks imaginable within the bounds of broadcast decency. Special effort was made to target audiences already on vacation at the shore. Moreover, the shore was where you could find, for the first time ever, an unprecedented array of licensed merchandise. First came the t-shirts, mugs, and beach bags featuring the famous poster of a young woman swimming obliviously, about to be devoured from below, and after that the fake plastic fins, sold in joke shops, broke all sales records. Soon, other brands and lobbies began to spoof the poster. Even political parties used it to demonize their opponents. *Jaws* was a hit like no other, becoming the first movie to earn the previously legendary $100,000 in ticket sales, far outstripping the recent successes of two other enfant terribles of New Hollywood, Francis Ford Coppola's *The Godfather* and William Friedkin's *The Exorcist*. In just the first six weeks of its release, one in eight Americans had seen *Jaws*. Steven Spielberg had just invented a terror machine.

KNOWLEDGE IS UNDERSTANDING

And so, in a few telling examples, we see why humans have too often been led to think of sharks as evil creatures. This wouldn't matter as much if many species of shark were not in danger of going extinct. But clichés can be long-lived. Scientists try to choose their words carefully—preferring, for instance, the word "encounter" for human-shark interactions rather than the word "attack[4]"—but they still have a hard time dispelling myths and falsehoods. And yet the evidence is clear: sharks do not enjoy eating humans. They've never liked hard-boned creatures, preferring the suppleness of, say, seals. That is why, in most cases, sharks will reject prey once they realize it's human. Which also explains why there are more cases of shark bites than fatalities. The comic you are about to read doesn't dwell on these issues. It even deliberately avoids anxiety-inducing scenarios. Instead, Bernard Séret takes a positive approach, showing why the reasons sharks have become the big baddies of the big blue are actually based on misconceptions and a lamentable lack of understanding.

David Vandermeulen

NOTES

1. Jacques-Yves Cousteau and Louis Malle, *The Silent World*, Cannes Film Festival Palme d'Or 1956, 00:56-00:59.

2. The story found a home in the famous monologue delivered by Quint the shark hunter, who in the movie was a survivor of the *Indianapolis*.

3. *Jaws* was so successful it propelled Verna Fields right into a vice-president position at Universal, making her one of the first women to occupy such a high-ranking post at a major studio.

4. These linguistic tactics are even more apt if we take into account the fact that most human-shark contact results from an accident or misunderstanding.

THE LITTLE BOOK

OF KNOWLEDGE:

SHARKS

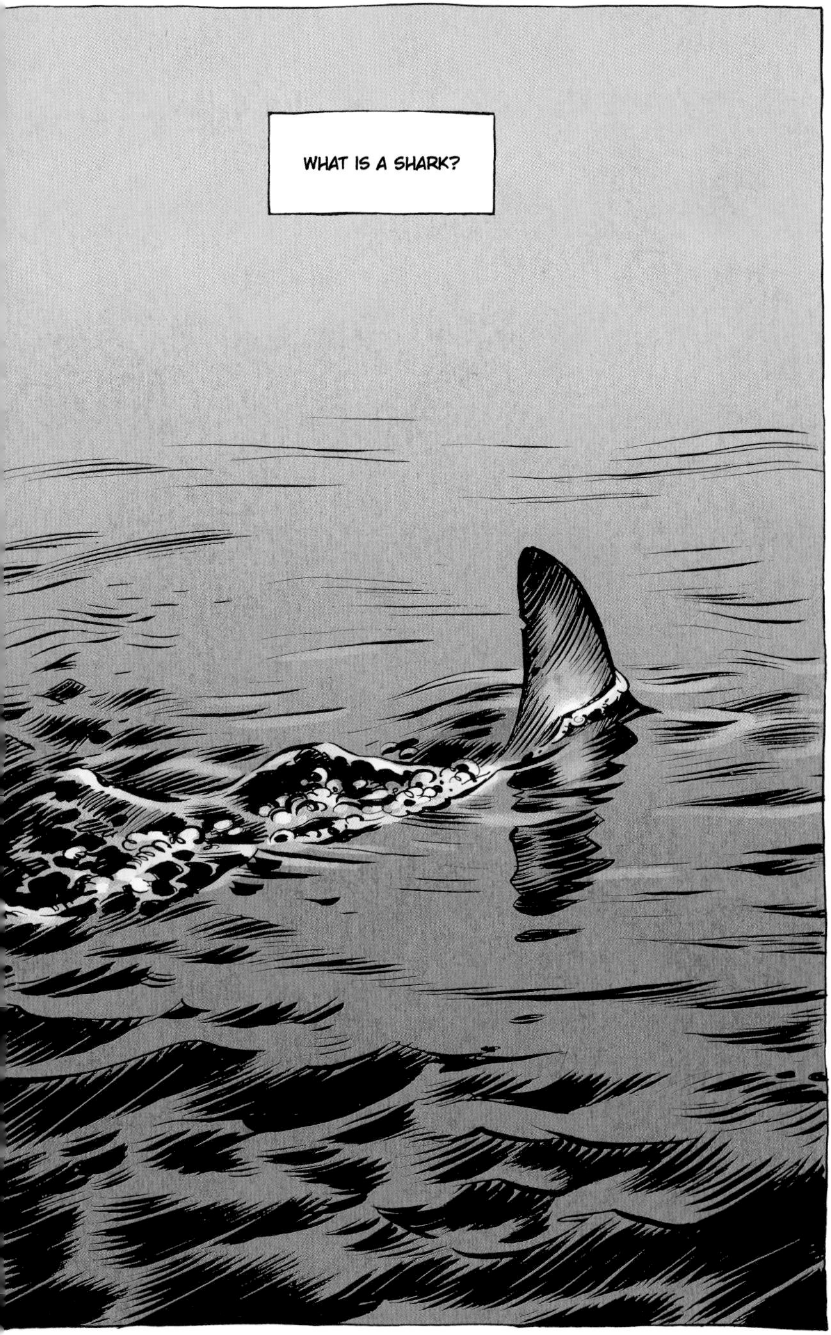
WHAT IS A SHARK?

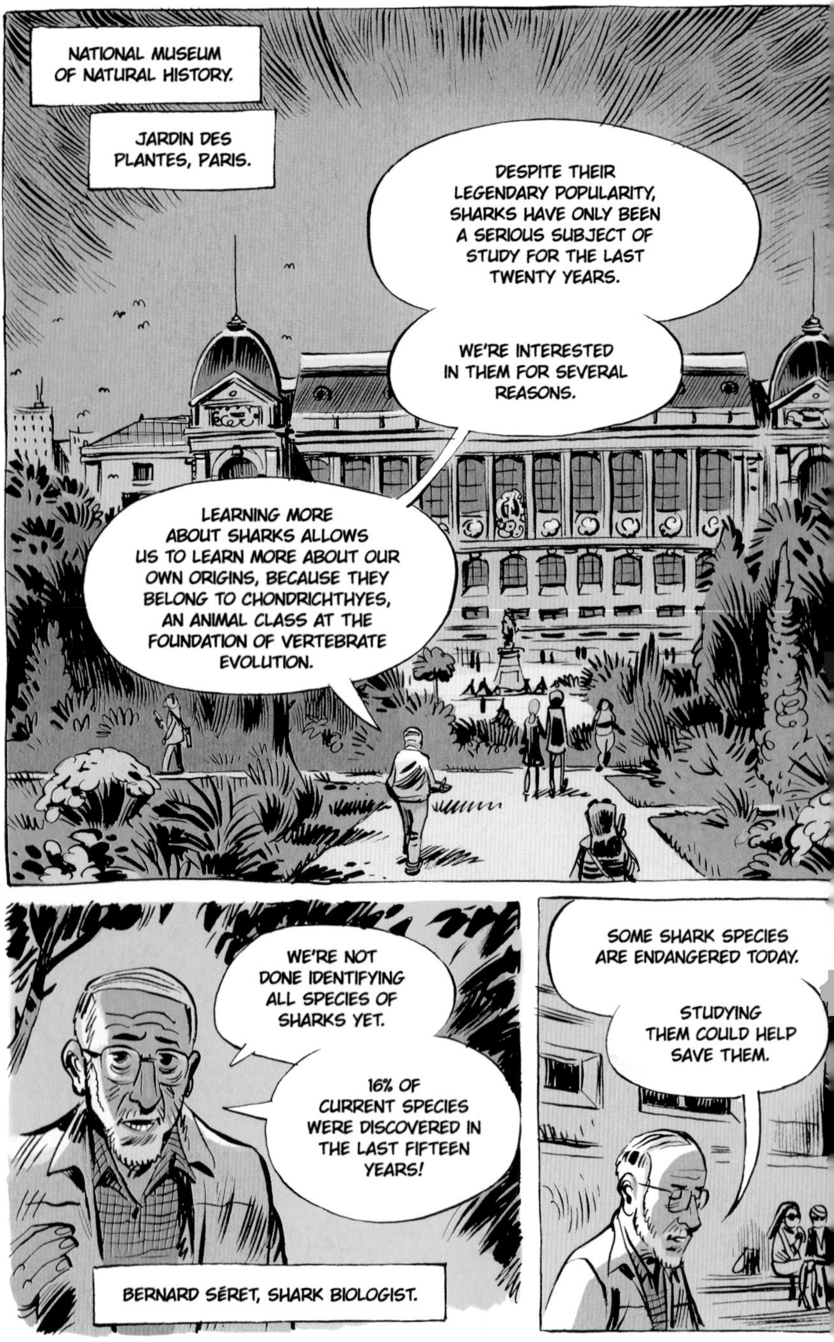
NATIONAL MUSEUM OF NATURAL HISTORY.
JARDIN DES PLANTES, PARIS.
DESPITE THEIR LEGENDARY POPULARITY, SHARKS HAVE ONLY BEEN A SERIOUS SUBJECT OF STUDY FOR THE LAST TWENTY YEARS.
WE'RE INTERESTED IN THEM FOR SEVERAL REASONS.
LEARNING MORE ABOUT SHARKS ALLOWS US TO LEARN MORE ABOUT OUR OWN ORIGINS, BECAUSE THEY BELONG TO CHONDRICHTHYES, AN ANIMAL CLASS AT THE FOUNDATION OF VERTEBRATE EVOLUTION.
WE'RE NOT DONE IDENTIFYING ALL SPECIES OF SHARKS YET.
16% OF CURRENT SPECIES WERE DISCOVERED IN THE LAST FIFTEEN YEARS!
BERNARD SÉRET, SHARK BIOLOGIST.
SOME SHARK SPECIES ARE ENDANGERED TODAY.
STUDYING THEM COULD HELP SAVE THEM.

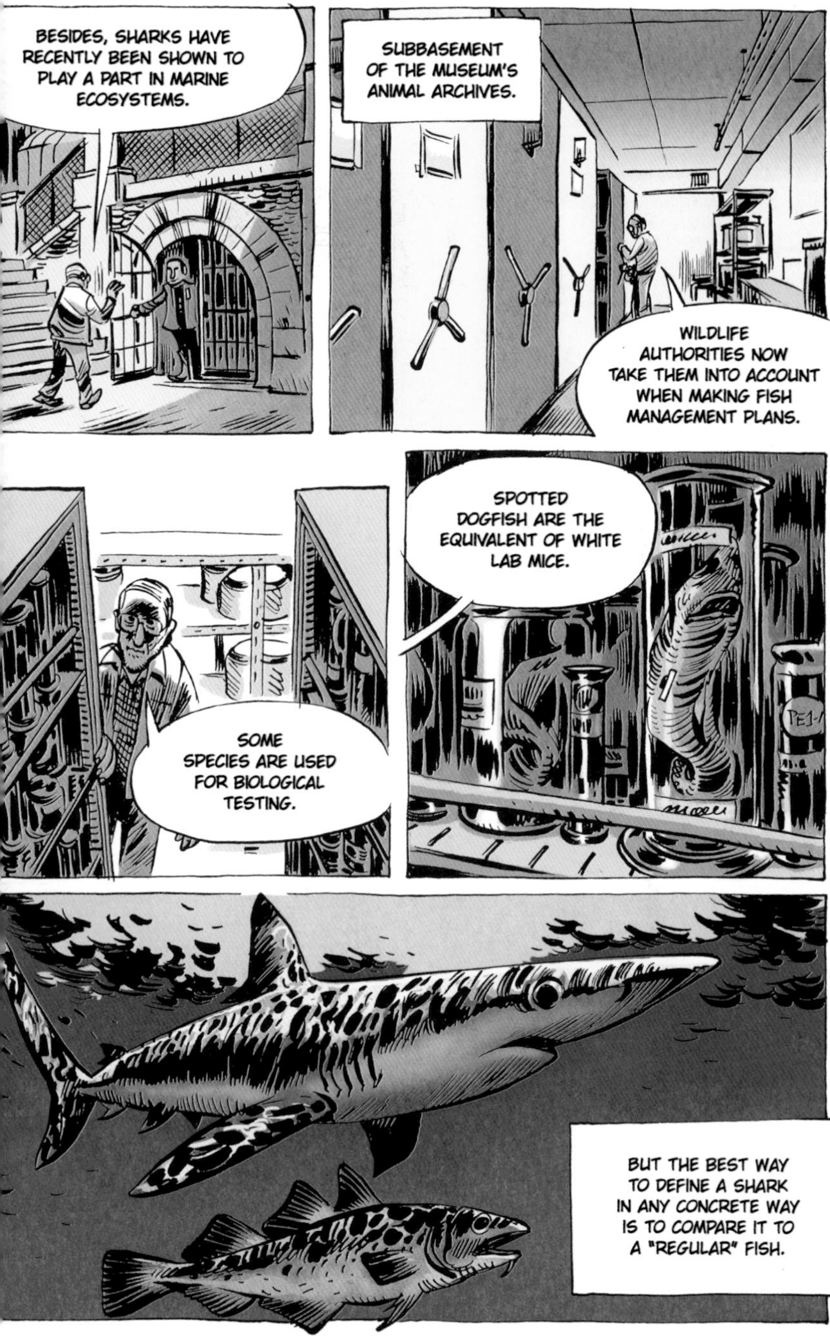
BESIDES, SHARKS HAVE RECENTLY BEEN SHOWN TO PLAY A PART IN MARINE ECOSYSTEMS.
SUBBASEMENT OF THE MUSEUM'S ANIMAL ARCHIVES.
WILDLIFE AUTHORITIES NOW TAKE THEM INTO ACCOUNT WHEN MAKING FISH MANAGEMENT PLANS.
SOME SPECIES ARE USED FOR BIOLOGICAL TESTING.
SPOTTED DOGFISH ARE THE EQUIVALENT OF WHITE LAB MICE.
BUT THE BEST WAY TO DEFINE A SHARK IN ANY CONCRETE WAY IS TO COMPARE IT TO A "REGULAR" FISH.

THE PRIMARY IDENTIFYING CHARACTERISTIC IS THE NATURE OF THE SKELETON. THERE ARE TWO MAIN GROUPS.

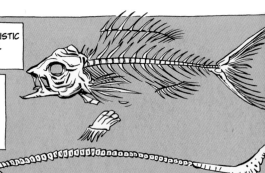

BONY FISHES (TUNA, SARDINES, SOLES, ETC.) AND CARTILAGINOUS FISHES (SHARKS, RAYS, AND CHIMAERAS).

CARTILAGE IS A LIGHT, SUPPLE MATERIAL—USEFUL PROPERTIES FOR A PREDATOR.

SHARKS HAVE TEETH!

BONY FISH DO TOO, BUT SHARK TEETH ARE IMPLANTED IN THE GUMS. THE FRONT ROWS OF TEETH ARE FUNCTIONAL, AND SERVE TO CAPTURE PREY.

WHEN THEY BREAK OR FALL OUT NATURALLY, THEY ARE REPLACED BY NEW TEETH "CONTINUOUSLY GROWING" FROM THE GUMS.

THE SYSTEM WORKS LIKE A MOVING WALKWAY. OVER THE COURSE OF ITS LIFE, A SHARK CAN PRODUCE THOUSANDS OF TEETH.

UNLIKE MOST BONY FISH, SHARKS HAVE NO SCALES, BUT THEIR SKINS ARE COVERED WITH MILLIONS OF TINY TOOTHLIKE STRUCTURES: DERMAL DENTICLES.

WITH BONY FISH, TEETH ARE IMPLANTED IN ALVEOLI, OR SOCKETS IN THE JAWBONE, JUST AS WITH HUMANS. THAT'S WHY IT HURTS SO MUCH WHEN THEY'RE PULLED!

DENTICLES ARE MINIATURE TEETH AND, LIKE TEETH, HAVE A CENTRAL PULP CAVITY, WITH NERVES AND BLOOD VESSELS. IN FACT, TEETH THEMSELVES ARE OVERDEVELOPED DENTICLES.

DENTICLES DO NOT GROW. THEY FALL OUT AND ARE REPLACED BY LARGER ONES.

WITH BONY FISH, SCALES GROW AS THE ANIMAL ITSELF GROWS. COUNTING THE RINGS ON A SCALE TELLS US A FISH'S AGE.

THE FINS OF BONY FISH ARE WEBS OF SKIN SUPPORTED BY BONY OR HORNY SPINES THAT ARE HIGHLY FLEXIBLE.

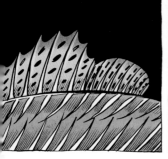

SHARK FINS ARE FLESHY AND FAIRLY RIGID. THEY ARE SUPPORTED BY CARTILAGINOUS RAYS AND FILAMENTS OF ELASTIC PROTEIN (WHICH ARE USED IN MAKING THE FAMOUS "SHARK FIN SOUP").

GILLS IN BONY FISH ARE COVERED BY A BONY OR MEMBRANOUS OPERCULLUM. IN SHARKS, GILL CLEFTS OPEN DIRECTLY TO THE EXTERIOR, A SERIES OF FIVE TO SEVEN PAIRS OF BRANCHIAL SLITS ON EITHER SIDE OF THE HEAD.

UNLIKE MOST BONY FISH, SHARKS HAVE NO SWIM BLADDERS TO HELP THEM FLOAT. INSTEAD, THEY HAVE ENORMOUS, OIL-RICH LIVERS THAT CONTRIBUTE TO BUOYANCY, IN ADDITION TO LIGHT SKELETONS THAT ARE MOSTLY CARTILAGE.

SHARK INTESTINES ARE VERY SHORT COMPARED TO THOSE OF BONY FISH, THANKS TO A SPECIAL SEGMENT, THE SPIRAL VALVE. THIS CONTAINS MULTIPLE TURNS OF THE INTESTINAL WALL, THUS INCREASING THE ABSORPTIVE SURFACE WITHOUT ADDING LENGTH.

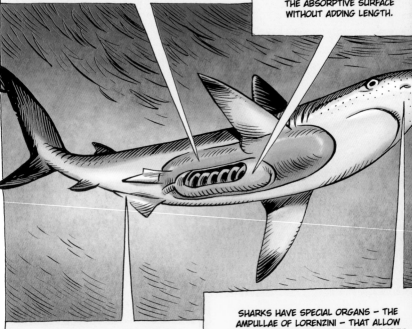

MALE SHARKS HAVE COPULATORY STRUCTURES CALLED CLASPERS, FORMED FROM THE POSTERIOR PART OF PELVIC FINS. SHARKS PRACTICE INTERNAL FERTILIZATION. A SINGLE FEMALE MAY MATE WITH ONE OR SEVERAL MALES: NO JUDGMENT!

SHARKS HAVE SPECIAL ORGANS – THE AMPULLAE OF LORENZINI – THAT ALLOW THEM TO DETECT WEAK ELECTROMAGNETIC FIELDS EMITTED BY LIVING PREY. LOOK AT A SHARK'S HEAD, ESPECIALLY THE VENTRAL SIDE, AND YOU'LL SEE A MULTITUDE OF TINY HOLES: THESE ARE THE AMPULLAE'S PORES. THE AMPULLAE THEMSELVES ARE BENEATH THE SKIN.

IF A FISH DISPLAYS ALL THESE FEATURES...

...AND A FEW OTHER HIDDEN ONES...

IT'S A SHARK!

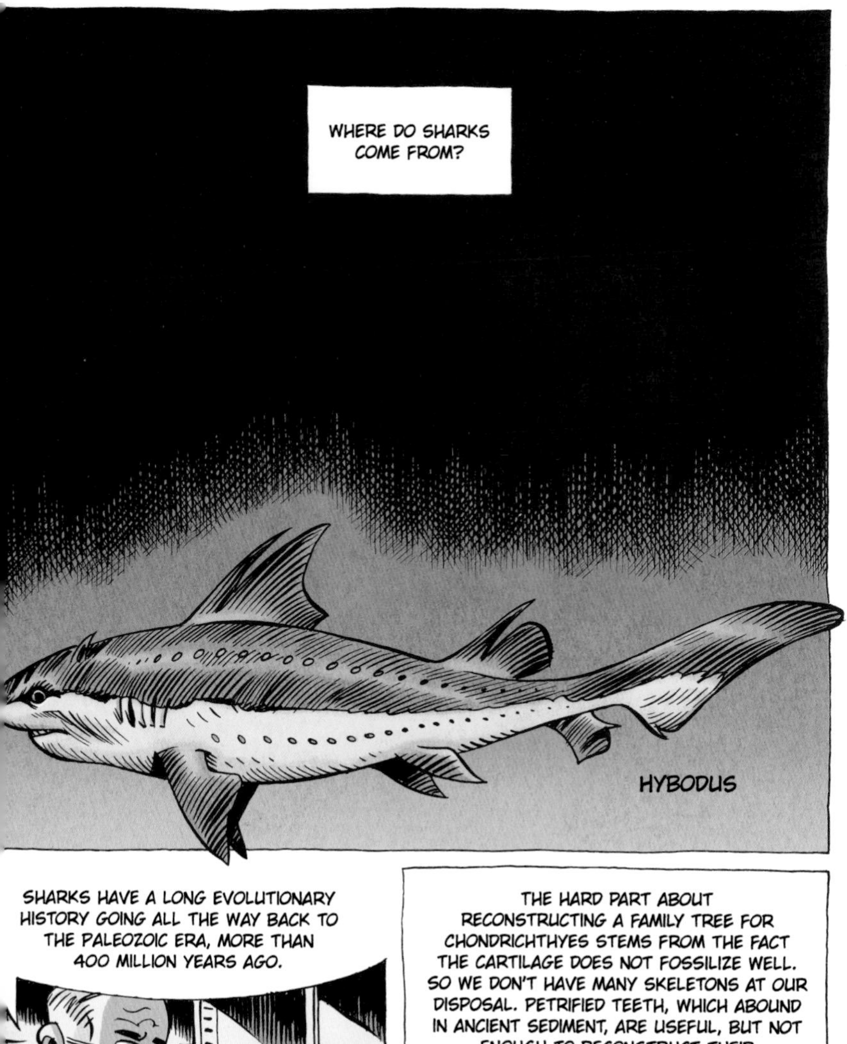
WHERE DO SHARKS COME FROM?
HYBODUS

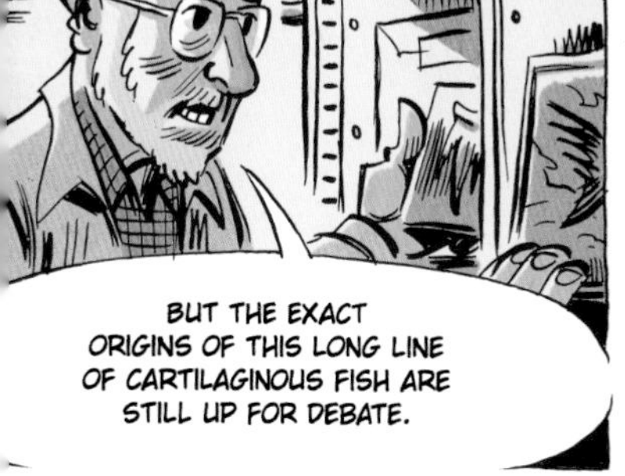
SHARKS HAVE A LONG EVOLUTIONARY HISTORY GOING ALL THE WAY BACK TO THE PALEOZOIC ERA, MORE THAN 400 MILLION YEARS AGO.
BUT THE EXACT ORIGINS OF THIS LONG LINE OF CARTILAGINOUS FISH ARE STILL UP FOR DEBATE.

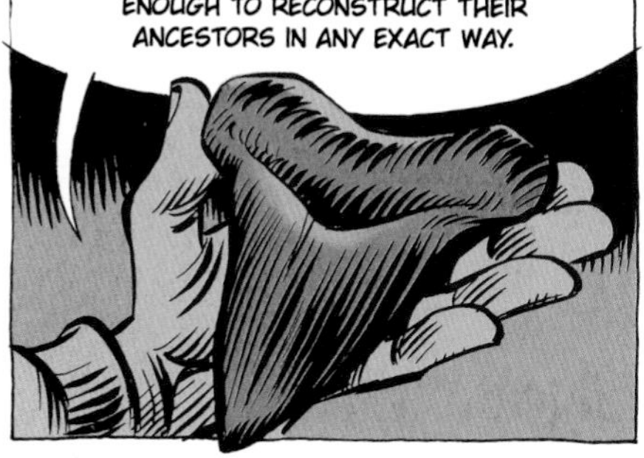
THE HARD PART ABOUT RECONSTRUCTING A FAMILY TREE FOR CHONDRICHTHYES STEMS FROM THE FACT THE CARTILAGE DOES NOT FOSSILIZE WELL. SO WE DON'T HAVE MANY SKELETONS AT OUR DISPOSAL. PETRIFIED TEETH, WHICH ABOUND IN ANCIENT SEDIMENT, ARE USEFUL, BUT NOT ENOUGH TO RECONSTRUCT THEIR ANCESTORS IN ANY EXACT WAY.

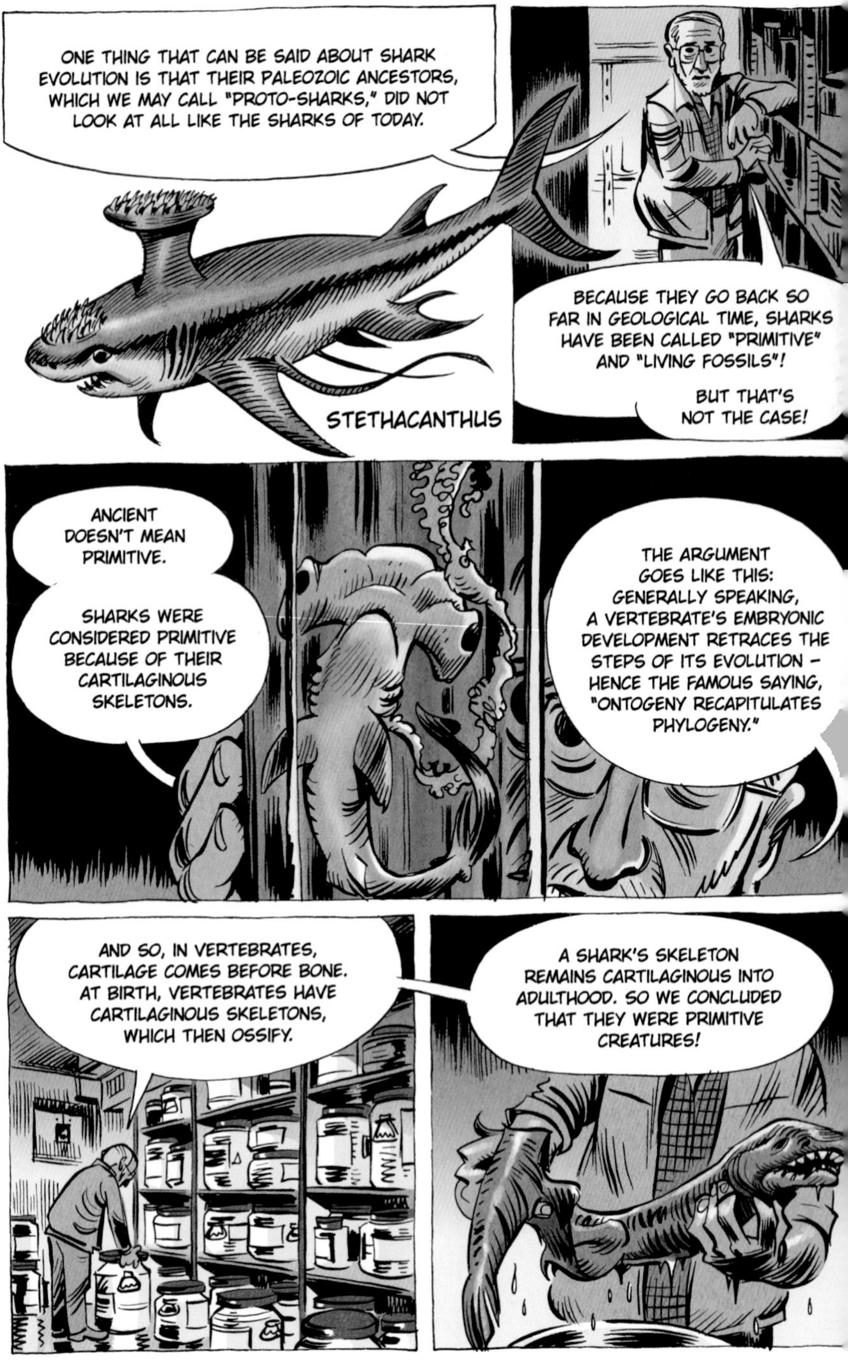

ONE THING THAT CAN BE SAID ABOUT SHARK EVOLUTION IS THAT THEIR PALEOZOIC ANCESTORS, WHICH WE MAY CALL "PROTO-SHARKS," DID NOT LOOK AT ALL LIKE THE SHARKS OF TODAY.

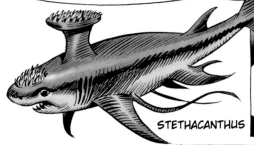

STETHACANTHUS

BECAUSE THEY GO BACK SO FAR IN GEOLOGICAL TIME, SHARKS HAVE BEEN CALLED "PRIMITIVE" AND "LIVING FOSSILS"!

BUT THAT'S NOT THE CASE!

ANCIENT DOESN'T MEAN PRIMITIVE.

SHARKS WERE CONSIDERED PRIMITIVE BECAUSE OF THEIR CARTILAGINOUS SKELETONS.

THE ARGUMENT GOES LIKE THIS: GENERALLY SPEAKING, A VERTEBRATE'S EMBRYONIC DEVELOPMENT RETRACES THE STEPS OF ITS EVOLUTION – HENCE THE FAMOUS SAYING, "ONTOGENY RECAPITULATES PHYLOGENY."

AND SO, IN VERTEBRATES, CARTILAGE COMES BEFORE BONE. AT BIRTH, VERTEBRATES HAVE CARTILAGINOUS SKELETONS, WHICH THEN OSSIFY.

A SHARK'S SKELETON REMAINS CARTILAGINOUS INTO ADULTHOOD. SO WE CONCLUDED THAT THEY WERE PRIMITIVE CREATURES!

N REALITY, THIS WAS AN ADAPTATION TO LIFE IN THE WATER.

SHARK SKELETONS GREW LIGHTER UNTIL THEY WERE COMPLETELY CARTILAGINOUS. THE RESULTING FLEXIBILITY WAS QUITE USEFUL FOR A PREDATOR.

SHARKS AREN'T "LIVING FOSSILS," EITHER. THEY'VE EVOLVED OVER THEIR LONG HISTORY. THIS HISTORY CAN BE SUMMED UP IN THREE MAJOR PERIODS.

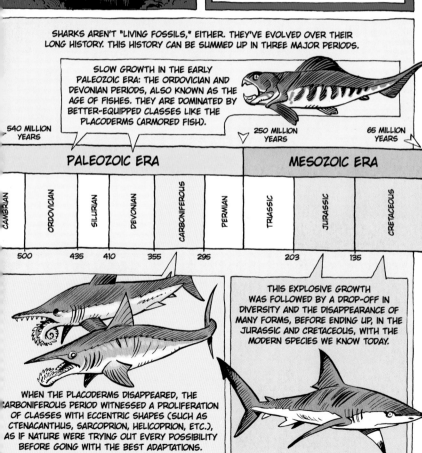

SLOW GROWTH IN THE EARLY PALEOZOIC ERA: THE ORDOVICIAN AND DEVONIAN PERIODS, ALSO KNOWN AS THE AGE OF FISHES. THEY ARE DOMINATED BY BETTER-EQUIPPED CLASSES LIKE THE PLACODERMS (ARMORED FISH).

540 MILLION YEARS

250 MILLION YEARS

65 MILLION YEARS

PALEOZOIC ERA

MESOZOIC ERA

CAMBRIAN	ORDOVICIAN	SILURIAN	DEVONIAN	CARBONIFEROUS	PERMIAN	TRIASSIC	JURASSIC	CRETACEOUS

500   435   410   355   295   203   135

WHEN THE PLACODERMS DISAPPEARED, THE CARBONIFEROUS PERIOD WITNESSED A PROLIFERATION OF CLASSES WITH ECCENTRIC SHAPES (SUCH AS CTENACANTHUS, SARCOPRION, HELICOPRION, ETC.), AS IF NATURE WERE TRYING OUT EVERY POSSIBILITY BEFORE GOING WITH THE BEST ADAPTATIONS.

THIS EXPLOSIVE GROWTH WAS FOLLOWED BY A DROP-OFF IN DIVERSITY AND THE DISAPPEARANCE OF MANY FORMS, BEFORE ENDING UP, IN THE JURASSIC AND CRETACEOUS, WITH THE MODERN SPECIES WE KNOW TODAY.

IN THIS LENGTHY EVOLUTIONARY HISTORY, THE FIRST GENUS TO LOOK ANYTHING LIKE A SHARK WERE THE CLADOSELACHES, WHICH APPEARED IN THE LATE DEVONIAN, 370 MILLION YEARS AGO. BUT THEY HAD TERMINAL MOUTHS (UNLIKE THE VENTRAL MOUTHS OF CURRENT SHARKS)...

...FEW DERMAL DENTICLES, AND THERE'S STILL SOME DOUBT AS TO WHETHER THEY HAD CLASPERS LIKE MODERN SHARKS—UNLESS WE WERE TO IMAGINE ALL THE FOSSIL SPECIMENS WE'VE FOUND TO DATE ARE FEMALE!

LET'S NOT FORGET SHARK "BRETHREN": RAYS AND CHIMAERAS.

RAYS ARE CLOSELY RELATED TO SHARKS.

LIKE SHARKS, RAYS HAVE CARTILAGINOUS SKELETONS. BUT THEIR BODIES ARE FLAT, AND AS A RESULT, THEIR GILL CLEFTS ARE ON THEIR VENTRAL SIDE. THEIR PECTORAL FINS ARE JOINED TO THEIR HEADS, FORMING A KIND OF DISC.

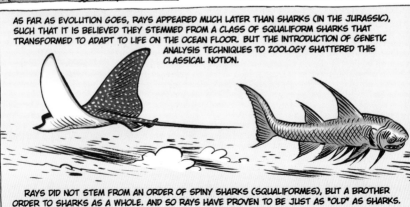

AS FAR AS EVOLUTION GOES, RAYS APPEARED MUCH LATER THAN SHARKS (IN THE JURASSIC), SUCH THAT IT IS BELIEVED THEY STEMMED FROM A CLASS OF SQUALIFORM SHARKS THAT TRANSFORMED TO ADAPT TO LIFE ON THE OCEAN FLOOR. BUT THE INTRODUCTION OF GENETIC ANALYSIS TECHNIQUES TO ZOOLOGY SHATTERED THIS CLASSICAL NOTION.

RAYS DID NOT STEM FROM AN ORDER OF SPINY SHARKS (SQUALIFORMES), BUT A BROTHER ORDER TO SHARKS AS A WHOLE. AND SO RAYS HAVE PROVEN TO BE JUST AS "OLD" AS SHARKS.

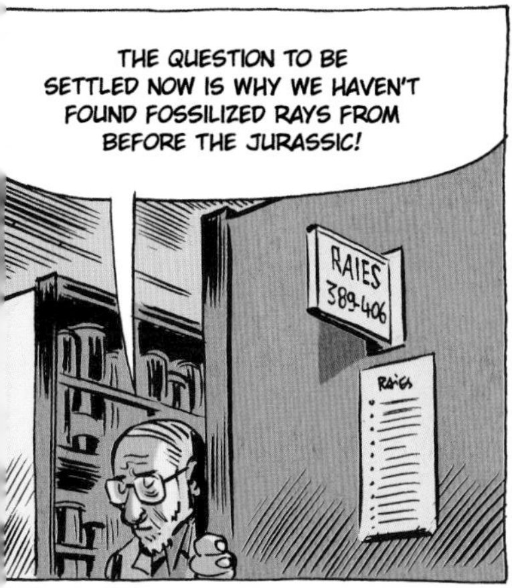
THE QUESTION TO BE SETTLED NOW IS WHY WE HAVEN'T FOUND FOSSILIZED RAYS FROM BEFORE THE JURASSIC!
RAIES
389-406
RAIES

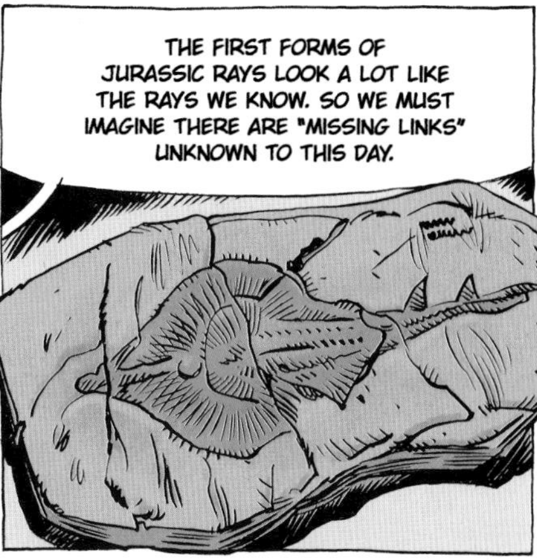
THE FIRST FORMS OF JURASSIC RAYS LOOK A LOT LIKE THE RAYS WE KNOW. SO WE MUST IMAGINE THERE ARE "MISSING LINKS" UNKNOWN TO THIS DAY.

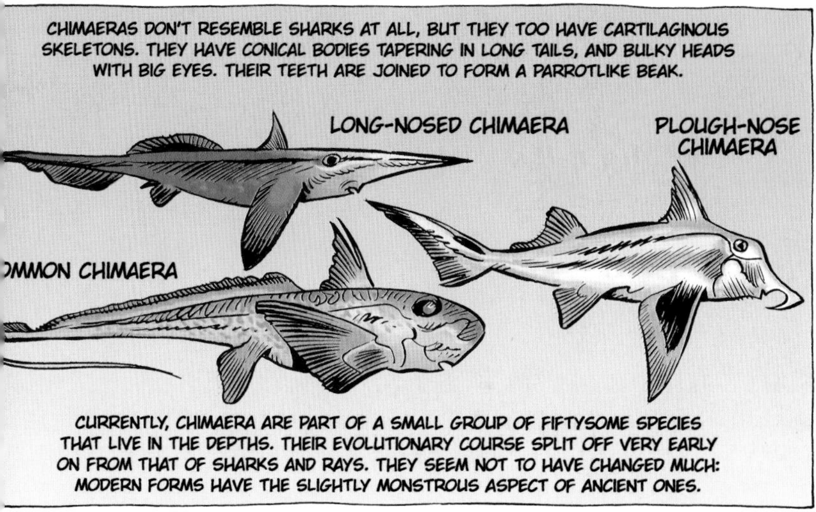
CHIMAERAS DON'T RESEMBLE SHARKS AT ALL, BUT THEY TOO HAVE CARTILAGINOUS SKELETONS. THEY HAVE CONICAL BODIES TAPERING IN LONG TAILS, AND BULKY HEADS WITH BIG EYES. THEIR TEETH ARE JOINED TO FORM A PARROTLIKE BEAK.
LONG-NOSED CHIMAERA
PLOUGH-NOSE CHIMAERA
OMMON CHIMAERA
CURRENTLY, CHIMAERA ARE PART OF A SMALL GROUP OF FIFTYSOME SPECIES THAT LIVE IN THE DEPTHS. THEIR EVOLUTIONARY COURSE SPLIT OFF VERY EARLY ON FROM THAT OF SHARKS AND RAYS. THEY SEEM NOT TO HAVE CHANGED MUCH: MODERN FORMS HAVE THE SLIGHTLY MONSTROUS ASPECT OF ANCIENT ONES.

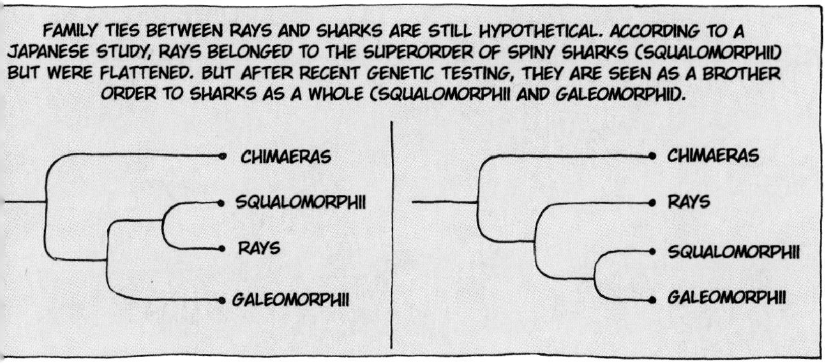
FAMILY TIES BETWEEN RAYS AND SHARKS ARE STILL HYPOTHETICAL. ACCORDING TO A JAPANESE STUDY, RAYS BELONGED TO THE SUPERORDER OF SPINY SHARKS (SQUALOMORPHII) BUT WERE FLATTENED. BUT AFTER RECENT GENETIC TESTING, THEY ARE SEEN AS A BROTHER ORDER TO SHARKS AS A WHOLE (SQUALOMORPHII AND GALEOMORPHII).
CHIMAERAS
SQUALOMORPHII
RAYS
GALEOMORPHII
CHIMAERAS
RAYS
SQUALOMORPHII
GALEOMORPHII

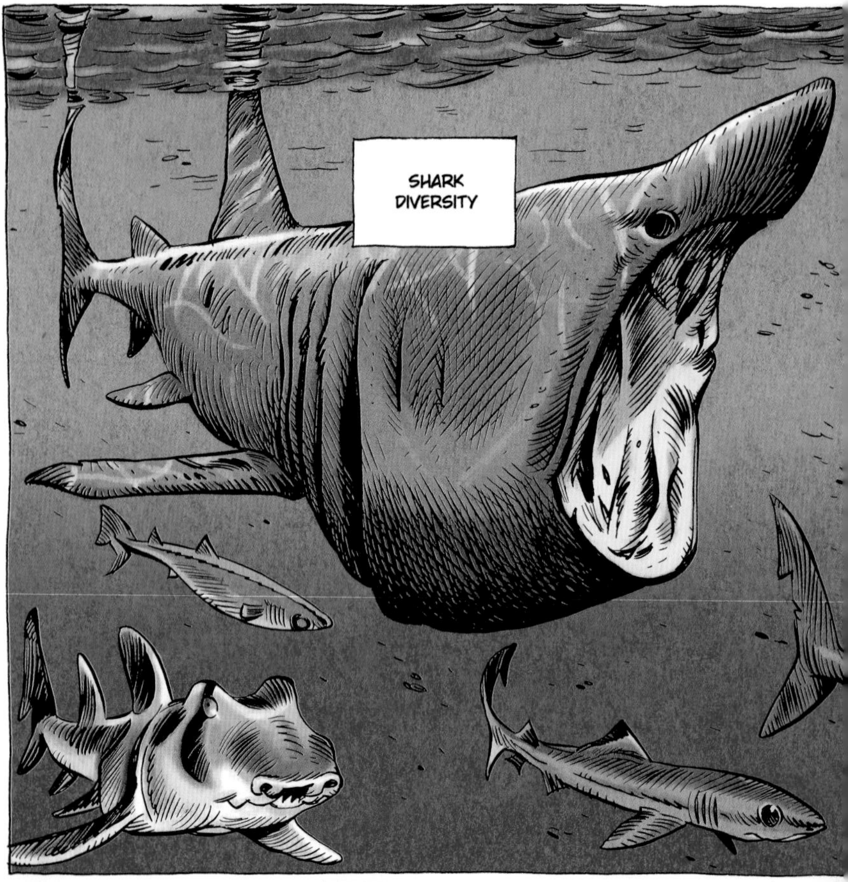
SHARK DIVERSITY

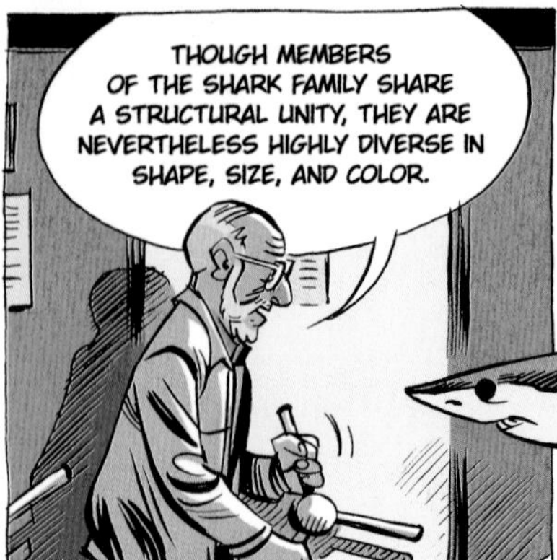
THOUGH MEMBERS OF THE SHARK FAMILY SHARE A STRUCTURAL UNITY, THEY ARE NEVERTHELESS HIGHLY DIVERSE IN SHAPE, SIZE, AND COLOR.

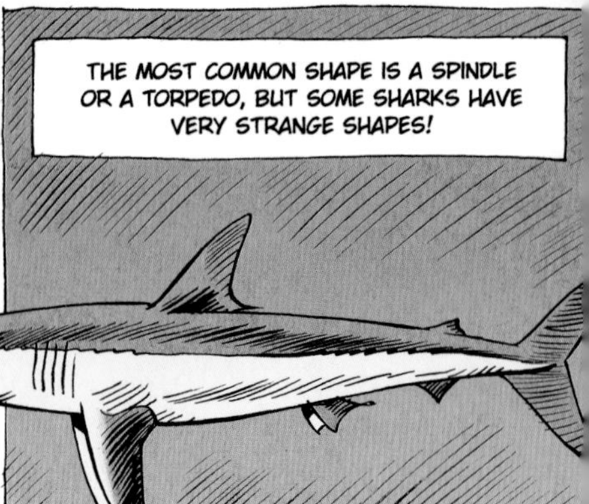
THE MOST COMMON SHAPE IS A SPINDLE OR A TORPEDO, BUT SOME SHARKS HAVE VERY STRANGE SHAPES!

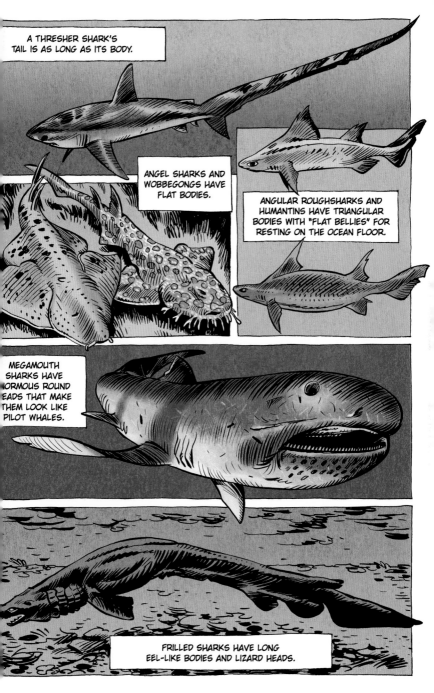

A THRESHER SHARK'S TAIL IS AS LONG AS ITS BODY.

ANGEL SHARKS AND WOBBEGONGS HAVE FLAT BODIES.

ANGULAR ROUGHSHARKS AND HUMANTINS HAVE TRIANGULAR BODIES WITH "FLAT BELLIES" FOR RESTING ON THE OCEAN FLOOR.

MEGAMOUTH SHARKS HAVE ENORMOUS ROUND HEADS THAT MAKE THEM LOOK LIKE PILOT WHALES.

FRILLED SHARKS HAVE LONG EEL-LIKE BODIES AND LIZARD HEADS.

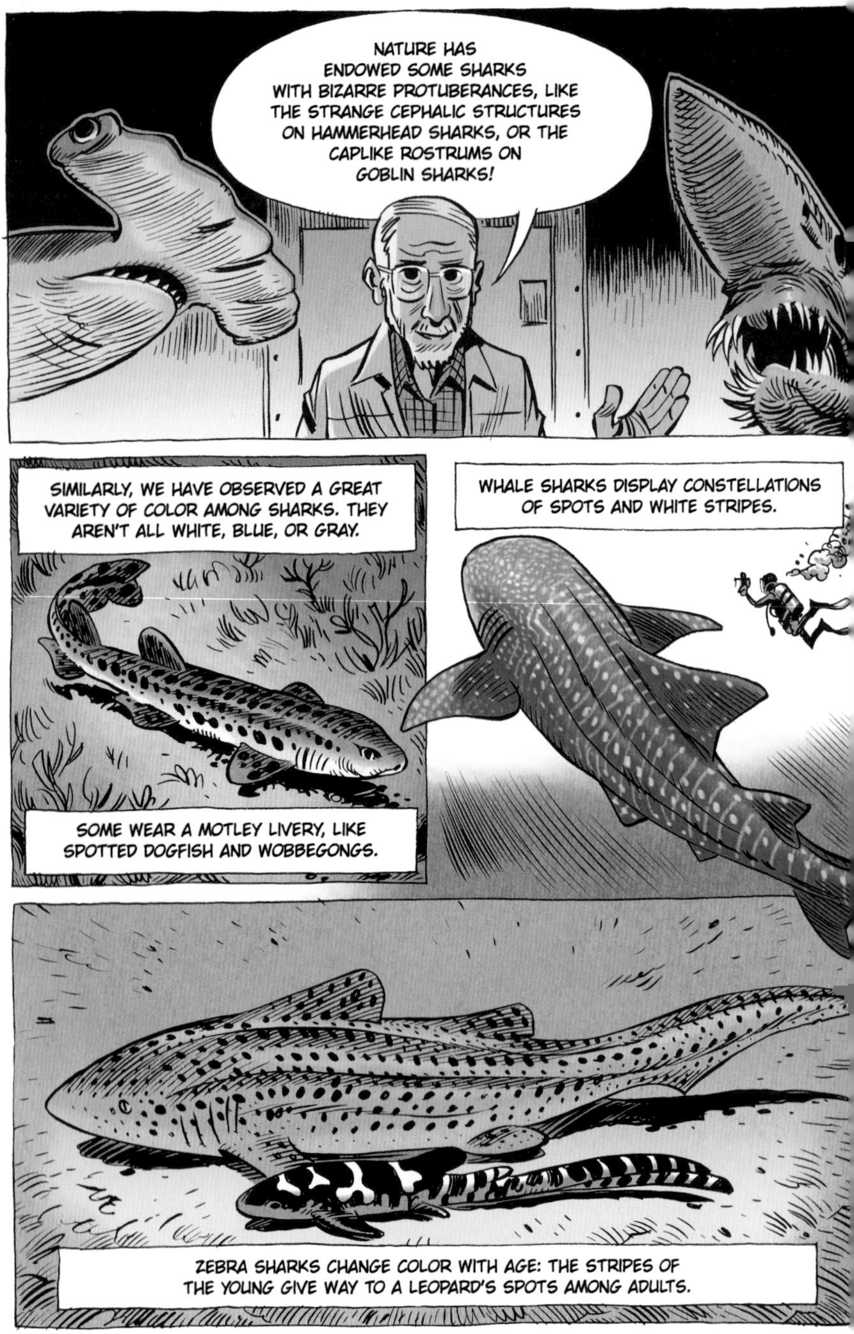
NATURE HAS ENDOWED SOME SHARKS WITH BIZARRE PROTUBERANCES, LIKE THE STRANGE CEPHALIC STRUCTURES ON HAMMERHEAD SHARKS, OR THE CAPLIKE ROSTRUMS ON GOBLIN SHARKS!
SIMILARLY, WE HAVE OBSERVED A GREAT VARIETY OF COLOR AMONG SHARKS. THEY AREN'T ALL WHITE, BLUE, OR GRAY.
SOME WEAR A MOTLEY LIVERY, LIKE SPOTTED DOGFISH AND WOBBEGONGS.
WHALE SHARKS DISPLAY CONSTELLATIONS OF SPOTS AND WHITE STRIPES.
ZEBRA SHARKS CHANGE COLOR WITH AGE: THE STRIPES OF THE YOUNG GIVE WAY TO A LEOPARD'S SPOTS AMONG ADULTS.

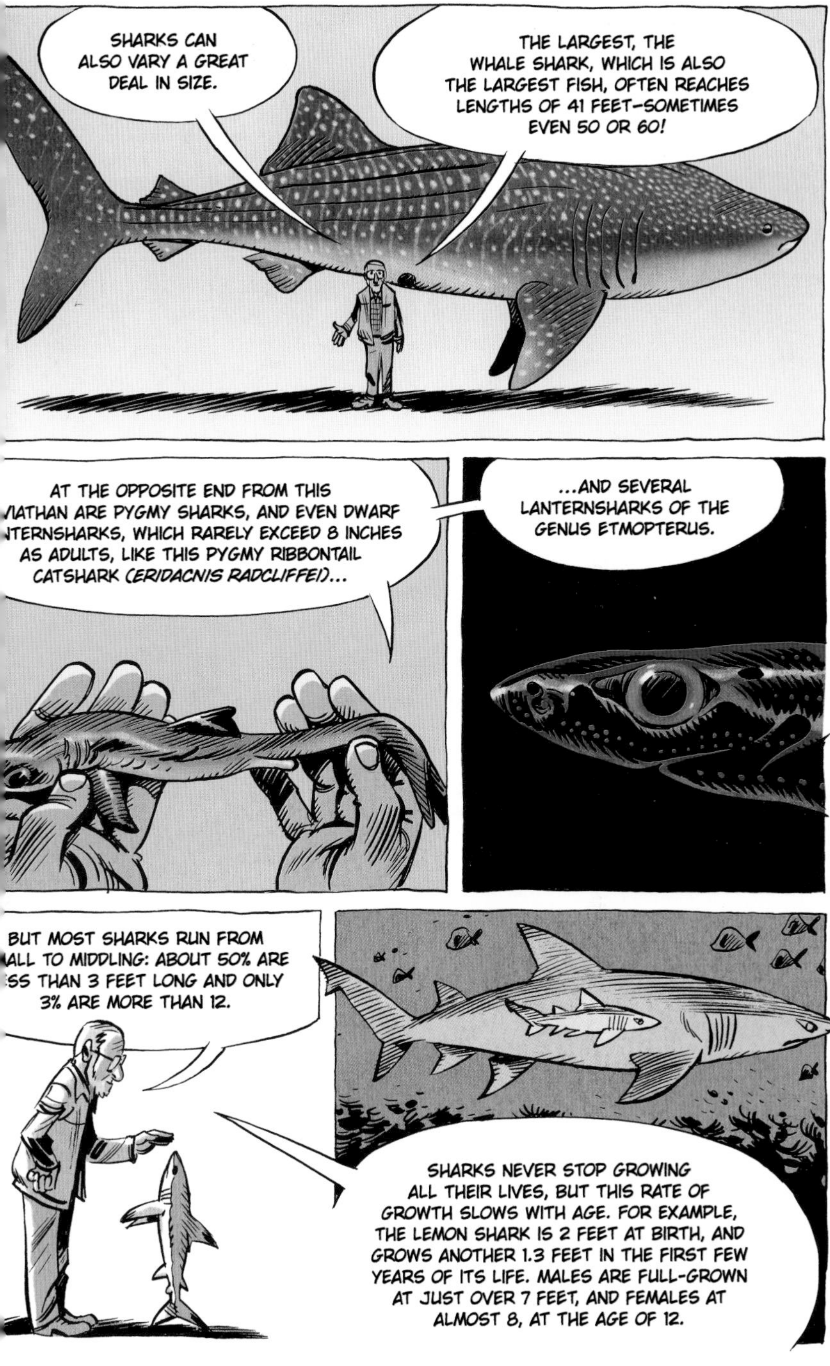

SHARKS CAN ALSO VARY A GREAT DEAL IN SIZE.

THE LARGEST, THE WHALE SHARK, WHICH IS ALSO THE LARGEST FISH, OFTEN REACHES LENGTHS OF 41 FEET—SOMETIMES EVEN 50 OR 60!

AT THE OPPOSITE END FROM THIS LEVIATHAN ARE PYGMY SHARKS, AND EVEN DWARF LANTERNSHARKS, WHICH RARELY EXCEED 8 INCHES AS ADULTS, LIKE THIS PYGMY RIBBONTAIL CATSHARK *(ERIDACNIS RADCLIFFEI)*...

...AND SEVERAL LANTERNSHARKS OF THE GENUS ETMOPTERUS.

BUT MOST SHARKS RUN FROM SMALL TO MIDDLING: ABOUT 50% ARE LESS THAN 3 FEET LONG AND ONLY 3% ARE MORE THAN 12.

SHARKS NEVER STOP GROWING ALL THEIR LIVES, BUT THIS RATE OF GROWTH SLOWS WITH AGE. FOR EXAMPLE, THE LEMON SHARK IS 2 FEET AT BIRTH, AND GROWS ANOTHER 1.3 FEET IN THE FIRST FEW YEARS OF ITS LIFE. MALES ARE FULL-GROWN AT JUST OVER 7 FEET, AND FEMALES AT ALMOST 8, AT THE AGE OF 12.

530 SPECIES OF SHARK HAVE BEEN DISCOVERED TO DATE.

IN 1984, WE'D ONLY DISCOVERED 380!

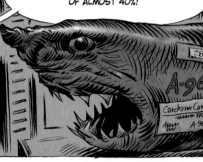

SO, 150 NEW SPECIES OF SHARKS WERE DISCOVERED AND CATALOGUED IN THE LAST 30 YEARS: AN INCREASE OF ALMOST 40%!

THIS BOOM IN SHARK DIVERSITY WAS THE RESULT OF GROWING INTEREST IN THIS FAMILY OF FISH...

...AND AN INTERNATIONAL EFFORT TO INVENTORY BIODIVERSITY, ESPECIALLY SEA LIFE, WHICH TOOK THE FORM OF MAJOR EXPLORATION CAMPAIGNS.

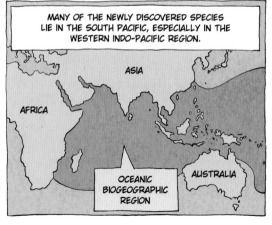

MANY OF THE NEWLY DISCOVERED SPECIES LIE IN THE SOUTH PACIFIC, ESPECIALLY IN THE WESTERN INDO-PACIFIC REGION.

ASIA

AFRICA

AUSTRALIA

OCEANIC BIOGEOGRAPHIC REGION

MOST WERE DEEP-WATER SPECIES, INHABITING ZONES AND DEPTHS RARELY EXPLORED IN THE PAST.

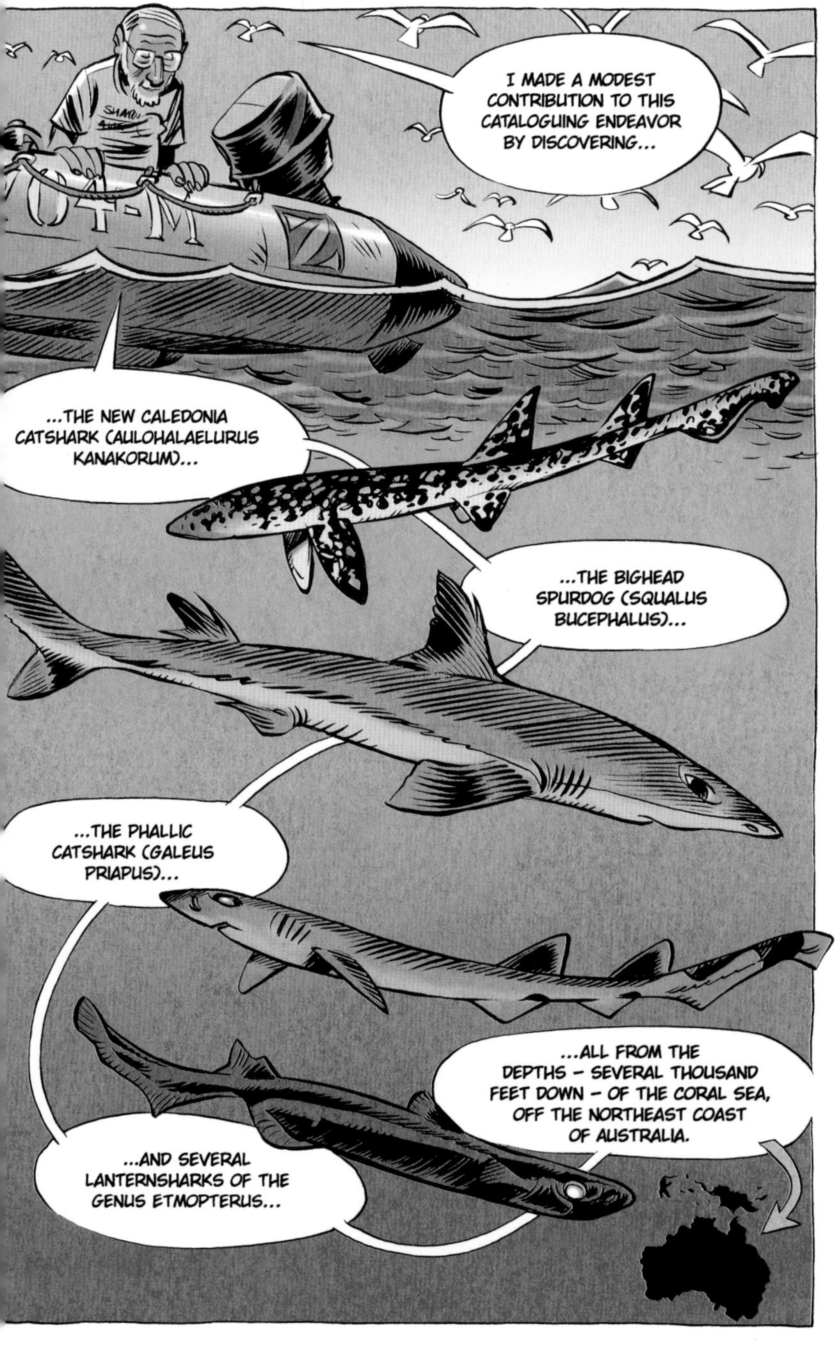
I MADE A MODEST CONTRIBUTION TO THIS CATALOGUING ENDEAVOR BY DISCOVERING...
...THE NEW CALEDONIA CATSHARK (AULOHALAELURUS KANAKORUM)...
...THE BIGHEAD SPURDOG (SQUALUS BUCEPHALUS)...
...THE PHALLIC CATSHARK (GALEUS PRIAPUS)...
...AND SEVERAL LANTERNSHARKS OF THE GENUS ETMOPTERUS...
...ALL FROM THE DEPTHS - SEVERAL THOUSAND FEET DOWN - OF THE CORAL SEA, OFF THE NORTHEAST COAST OF AUSTRALIA.

THE RECENT INTRODUCTION OF GENETIC ANALYSIS TECHNIQUES TO ZOOLOGY PLAYED A PART IN AUGMENTING THE SPECIES COUNT.

THESE POWERFUL TECHNIQUES ALLOW US TO DIFFERENTIATE SPECIES IN COMPLEX CASES WHERE TRADITIONAL COMPARATIVE ANATOMY WOULD HAVE STRUGGLED.

BUT GENETIC ANALYSIS HAS ITS OWN PRACTICAL DIFFICULTIES: THERE ARE CASES WHERE SUCH TECHNIQUES DISTINGUISH SPECIES THAT ARE MORPHOLOGICALLY INDIFFERENTIABLE, AND VICE VERSA.

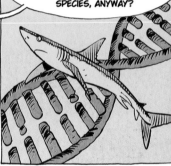

WHAT'S MORE, CERTAIN SHARKS ARE ABLE TO CROSS-BREED, WHICH BRINGS UP THE PERENNIAL QUESTION: JUST HOW DO WE DEFINE A SPECIES, ANYWAY?

FOR ALL THESE REASONS, IT IS IMPORTANT TO SPEAK OF SHARKS AS IF THERE WERE ONLY ONE KIND, MYTHICAL AND STEREOTYPICAL IN WAYS FAR REMOVED FROM REALITY!

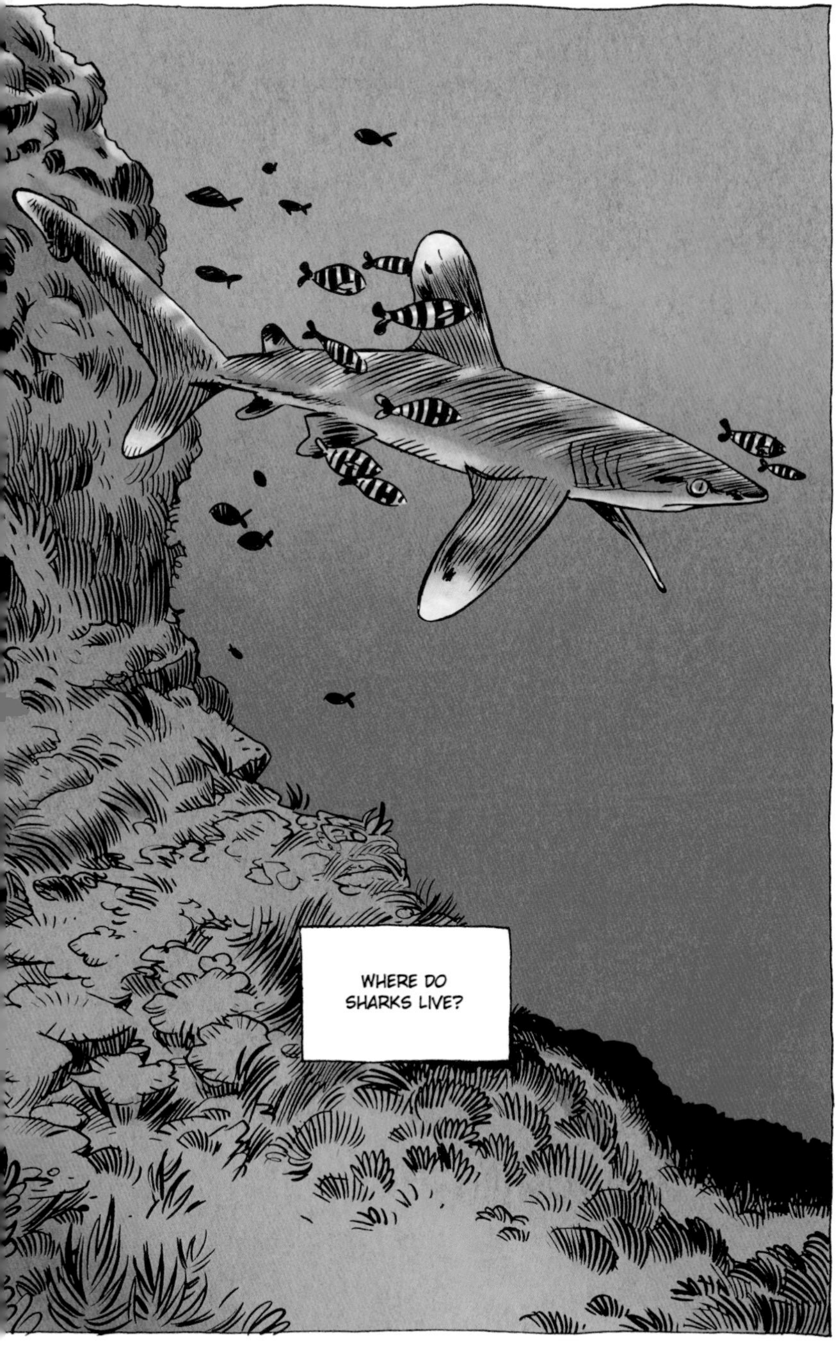
WHERE DO SHARKS LIVE?

IN THE POPULAR IMAGINATION, SHARKS ARE GENERALLY ASSOCIATED WITH WARM TROPICAL WATERS.

TRUE, THEY ARE MORE DIVERSE AND PLENTIFUL IN WARM WATERS.

BUT THERE ARE ALSO SHARKS IN TEMPERATE, COLD, AND EVEN POLAR WATERS! FOR EXAMPLE THE LAST CENSUS IN THE TEMPERATE WATERS O THE NORTHEAST ATLANTIC RECORDED OVER 80 SPECIES OF SHARKS.

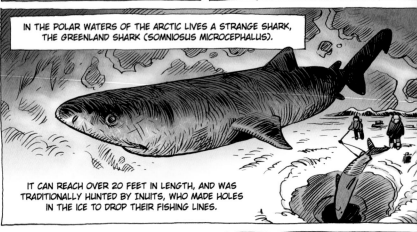

IN THE POLAR WATERS OF THE ARCTIC LIVES A STRANGE SHARK, THE GREENLAND SHARK (SOMNIOSUS MICROCEPHALUS).

IT CAN REACH OVER 20 FEET IN LENGTH, AND WAS TRADITIONALLY HUNTED BY INUITS, WHO MADE HOLES IN THE ICE TO DROP THEIR FISHING LINES.

SINCE THE FLESH OF THIS SHARK WAS NATURALLY TOXIC DUE TO HIGH CONCENTRATIONS OF TRIMETHYLAMINE OXIDE, IT WAS OFTEN FERMENTED PRIOR TO CONSUMPTION.

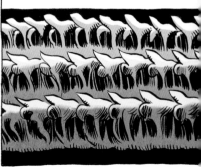

THE SAWLIKE TEETH OF ITS LOWER JAW WERE USED AS RAZORS TO CUT WOMEN'S HAIR!

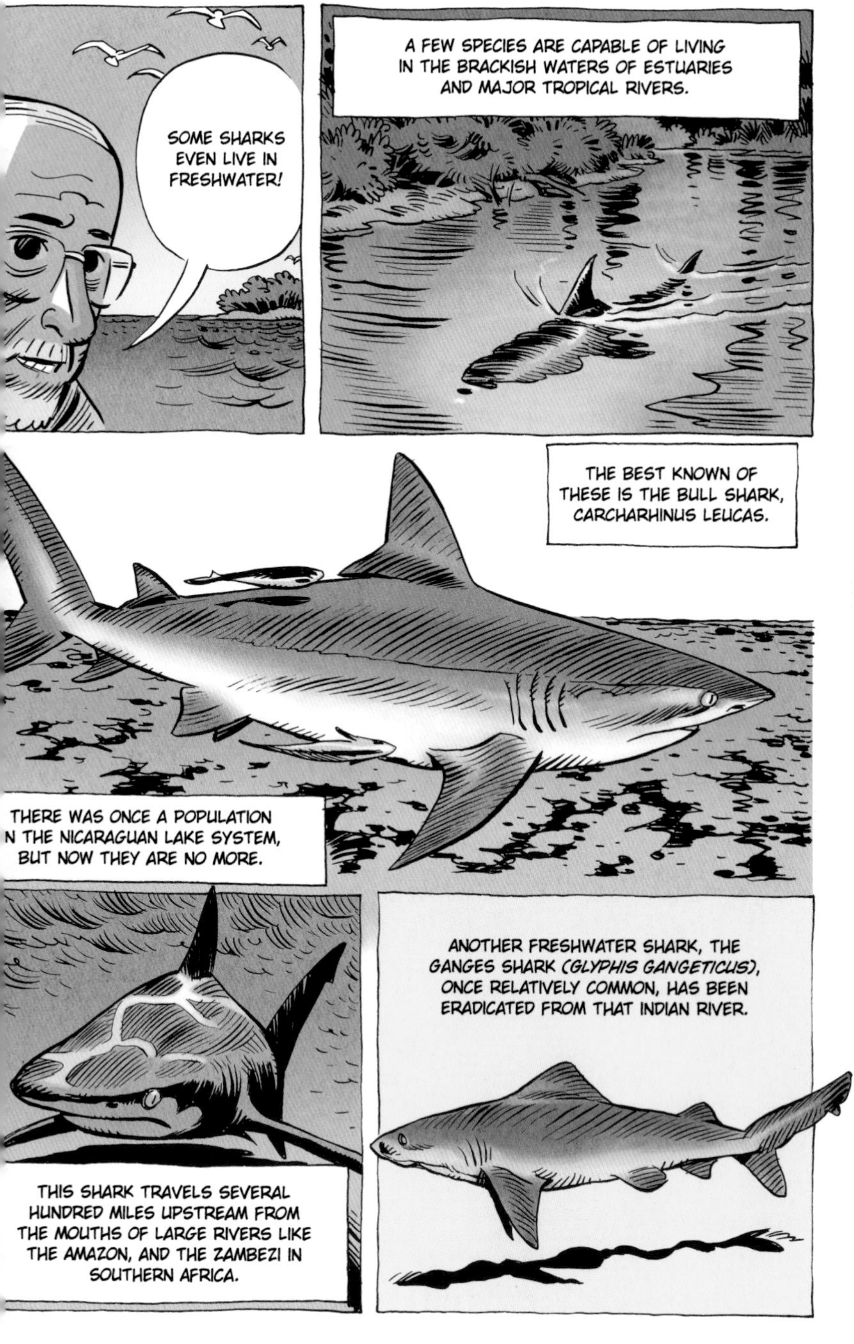
SOME SHARKS EVEN LIVE IN FRESHWATER!
A FEW SPECIES ARE CAPABLE OF LIVING IN THE BRACKISH WATERS OF ESTUARIES AND MAJOR TROPICAL RIVERS.
THE BEST KNOWN OF THESE IS THE BULL SHARK, CARCHARHINUS LEUCAS.
THERE WAS ONCE A POPULATION N THE NICARAGUAN LAKE SYSTEM, BUT NOW THEY ARE NO MORE.
THIS SHARK TRAVELS SEVERAL HUNDRED MILES UPSTREAM FROM THE MOUTHS OF LARGE RIVERS LIKE THE AMAZON, AND THE ZAMBEZI IN SOUTHERN AFRICA.
ANOTHER FRESHWATER SHARK, THE GANGES SHARK (*GLYPHIS GANGETICUS*), ONCE RELATIVELY COMMON, HAS BEEN ERADICATED FROM THAT INDIAN RIVER.

AT SEA, SHARKS CAN BE FOUND ALL OVER. THEIR BATHYMETRIC DISTRIBUTION RANGES FROM COASTAL WATERS ALL THE WAY TO THE ABYSSAL ZONE.

THE RECORD DEPTH FOR A SHARK – JUST UNDER 13,123 FEET! – IS HELD BY THE PORTUGUESE DOGFISH (CENTROSCYMNUS COELOLEPIS), A MEDIUM-SIZED SHARK OF ABOUT 4 FT., FAIRLY COSMOPOLITAN IN DISTRIBUTION.

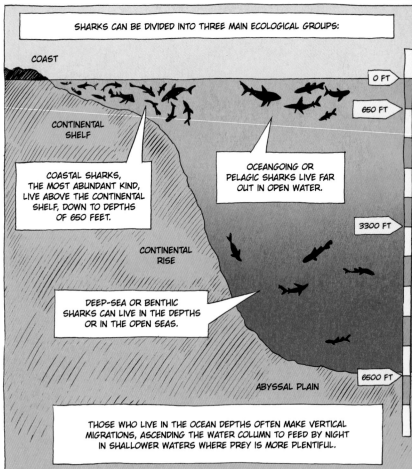

SHARKS CAN BE DIVIDED INTO THREE MAIN ECOLOGICAL GROUPS:

COAST

CONTINENTAL SHELF

0 FT

650 FT

COASTAL SHARKS, THE MOST ABUNDANT KIND, LIVE ABOVE THE CONTINENTAL SHELF, DOWN TO DEPTHS OF 650 FEET.

OCEANGOING OR PELAGIC SHARKS LIVE FAR OUT IN OPEN WATER.

CONTINENTAL RISE

3300 FT

DEEP-SEA OR BENTHIC SHARKS CAN LIVE IN THE DEPTHS OR IN THE OPEN SEAS.

ABYSSAL PLAIN

6500 FT

THOSE WHO LIVE IN THE OCEAN DEPTHS OFTEN MAKE VERTICAL MIGRATIONS, ASCENDING THE WATER COLUMN TO FEED BY NIGHT IN SHALLOWER WATERS WHERE PREY IS MORE PLENTIFUL.

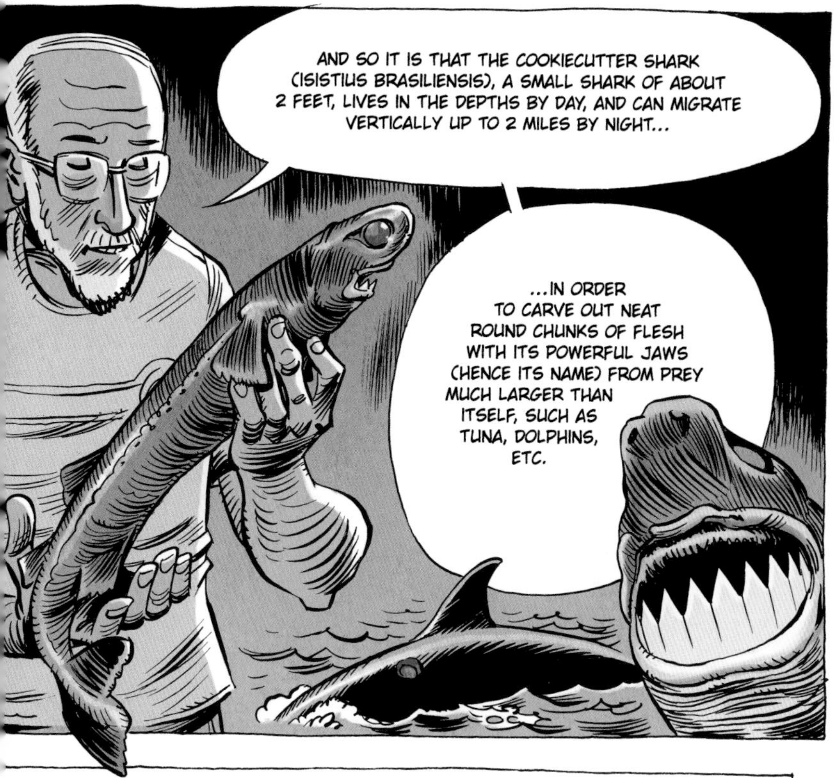
AND SO IT IS THAT THE COOKIECUTTER SHARK (ISISTIUS BRASILIENSIS), A SMALL SHARK OF ABOUT 2 FEET, LIVES IN THE DEPTHS BY DAY, AND CAN MIGRATE VERTICALLY UP TO 2 MILES BY NIGHT...
...IN ORDER TO CARVE OUT NEAT ROUND CHUNKS OF FLESH WITH ITS POWERFUL JAWS (HENCE ITS NAME) FROM PREY MUCH LARGER THAN ITSELF, SUCH AS TUNA, DOLPHINS, ETC.

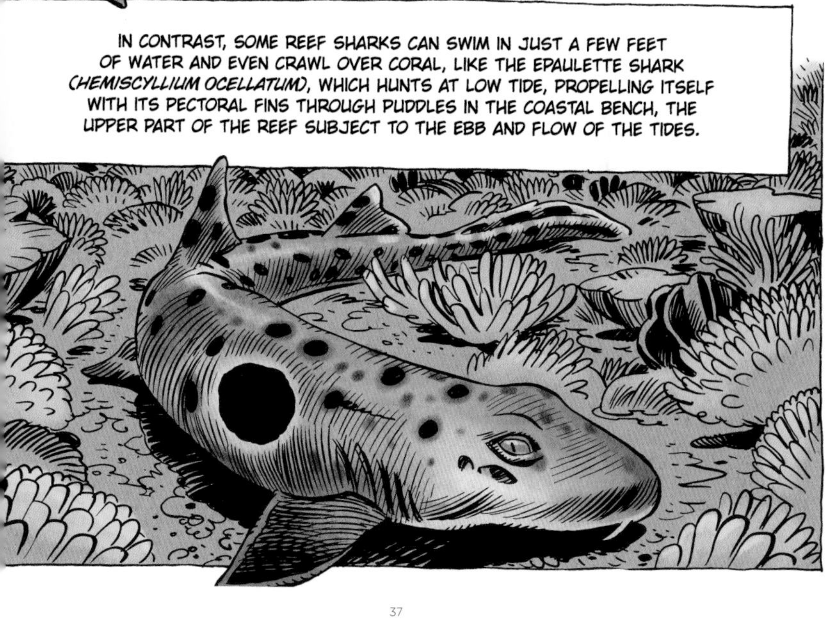
IN CONTRAST, SOME REEF SHARKS CAN SWIM IN JUST A FEW FEET OF WATER AND EVEN CRAWL OVER CORAL, LIKE THE EPAULETTE SHARK (*HEMISCYLLIUM OCELLATUM*), WHICH HUNTS AT LOW TIDE, PROPELLING ITSELF WITH ITS PECTORAL FINS THROUGH PUDDLES IN THE COASTAL BENCH, THE UPPER PART OF THE REEF SUBJECT TO THE EBB AND FLOW OF THE TIDES.

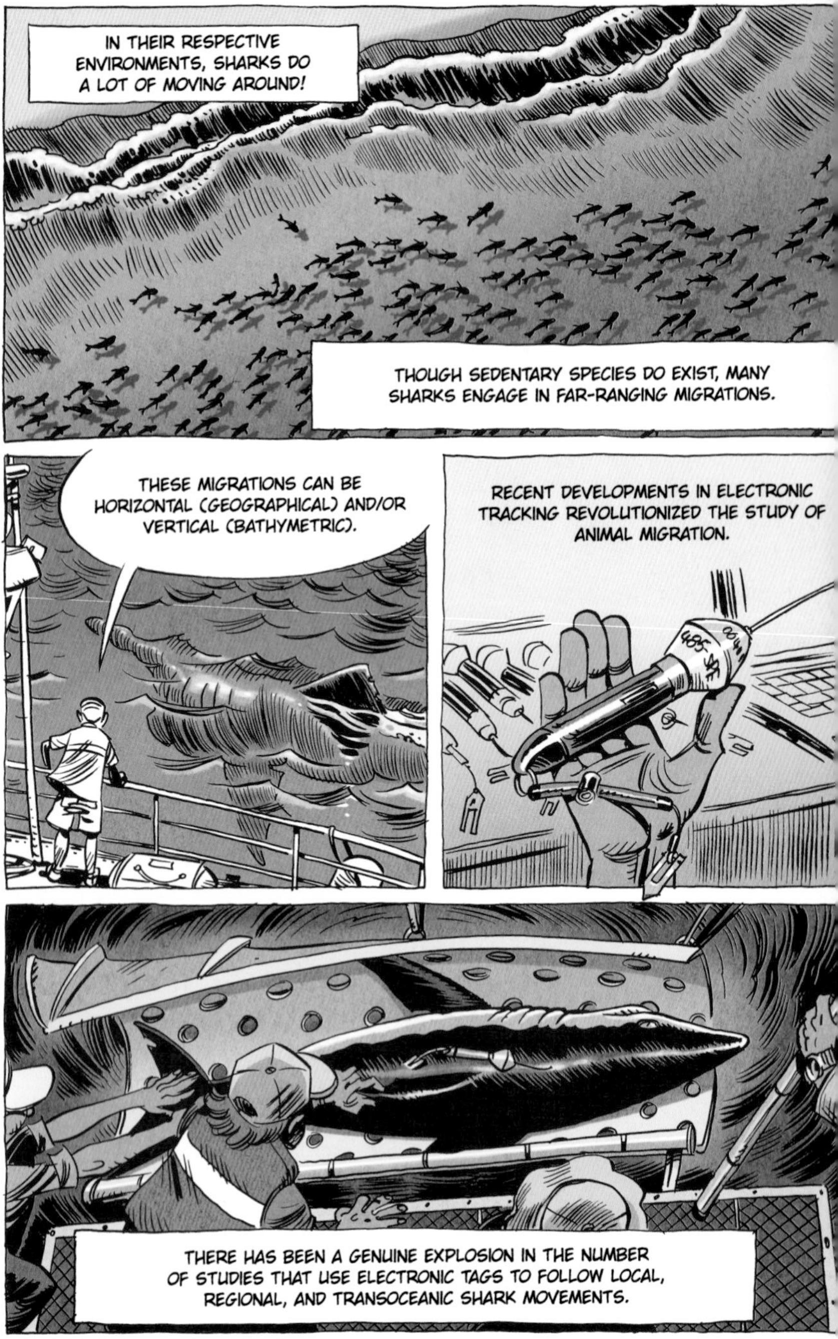
IN THEIR RESPECTIVE ENVIRONMENTS, SHARKS DO A LOT OF MOVING AROUND!
THOUGH SEDENTARY SPECIES DO EXIST, MANY SHARKS ENGAGE IN FAR-RANGING MIGRATIONS.
THESE MIGRATIONS CAN BE HORIZONTAL (GEOGRAPHICAL) AND/OR VERTICAL (BATHYMETRIC).
RECENT DEVELOPMENTS IN ELECTRONIC TRACKING REVOLUTIONIZED THE STUDY OF ANIMAL MIGRATION.
THERE HAS BEEN A GENUINE EXPLOSION IN THE NUMBER OF STUDIES THAT USE ELECTRONIC TAGS TO FOLLOW LOCAL, REGIONAL, AND TRANSOCEANIC SHARK MOVEMENTS.

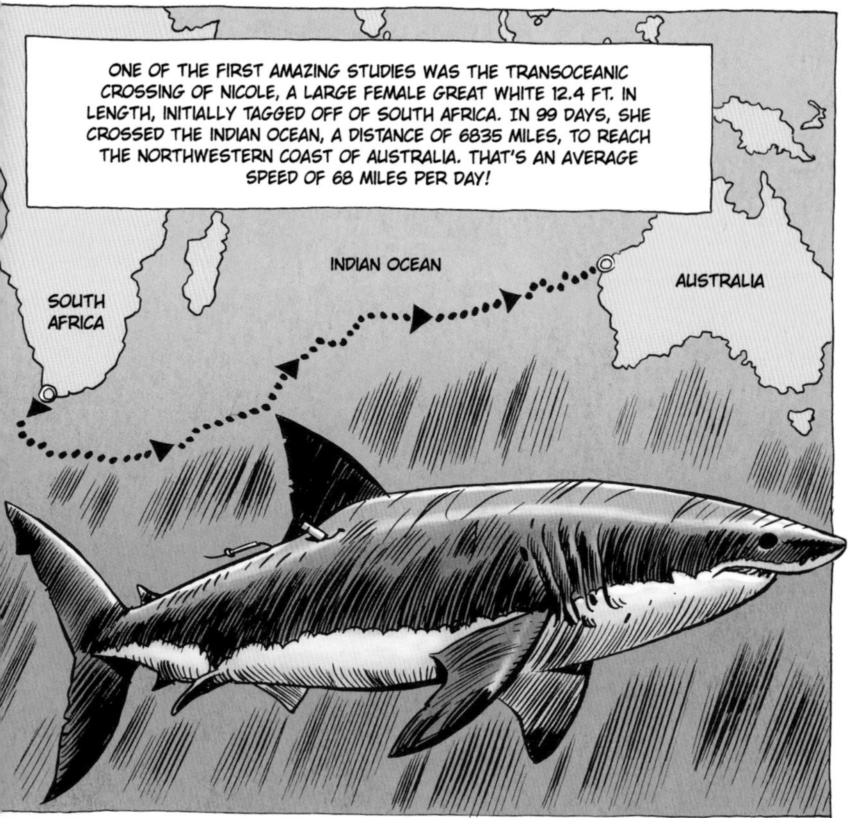
ONE OF THE FIRST AMAZING STUDIES WAS THE TRANSOCEANIC CROSSING OF NICOLE, A LARGE FEMALE GREAT WHITE 12.4 FT. IN LENGTH, INITIALLY TAGGED OFF OF SOUTH AFRICA. IN 99 DAYS, SHE CROSSED THE INDIAN OCEAN, A DISTANCE OF 6835 MILES, TO REACH THE NORTHWESTERN COAST OF AUSTRALIA. THAT'S AN AVERAGE SPEED OF 68 MILES PER DAY!
INDIAN OCEAN
SOUTH AFRICA
AUSTRALIA

URING HER VOYAGE, NICOLE MOST OFTEN SWAM NEAR THE SURFACE, BUT REGULARLY MADE DIVES OF 1/3 TO 2/3 OF A MILE DOWN. SHE THEN RETURNED TO SOUTH AFRICA NINE MONTHS LATER.

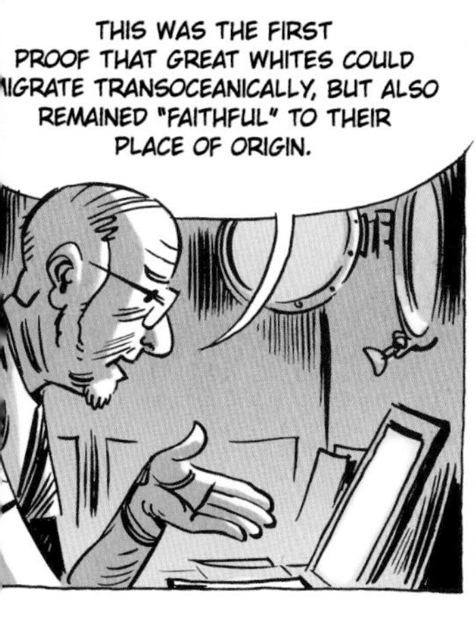
THIS WAS THE FIRST PROOF THAT GREAT WHITES COULD IGRATE TRANSOCEANICALLY, BUT ALSO REMAINED "FAITHFUL" TO THEIR PLACE OF ORIGIN.

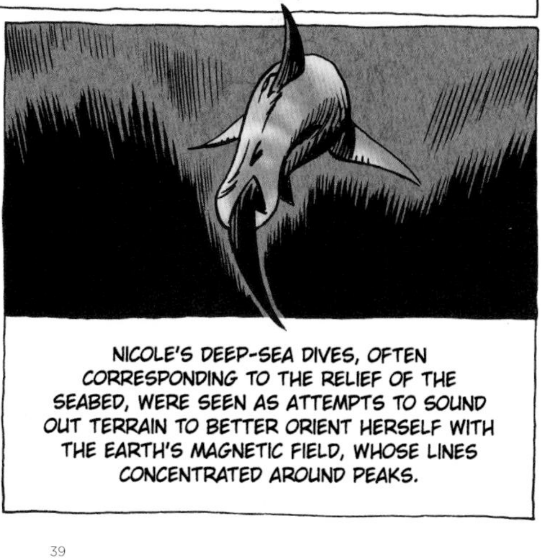
NICOLE'S DEEP-SEA DIVES, OFTEN CORRESPONDING TO THE RELIEF OF THE SEABED, WERE SEEN AS ATTEMPTS TO SOUND OUT TERRAIN TO BETTER ORIENT HERSELF WITH THE EARTH'S MAGNETIC FIELD, WHOSE LINES CONCENTRATED AROUND PEAKS.

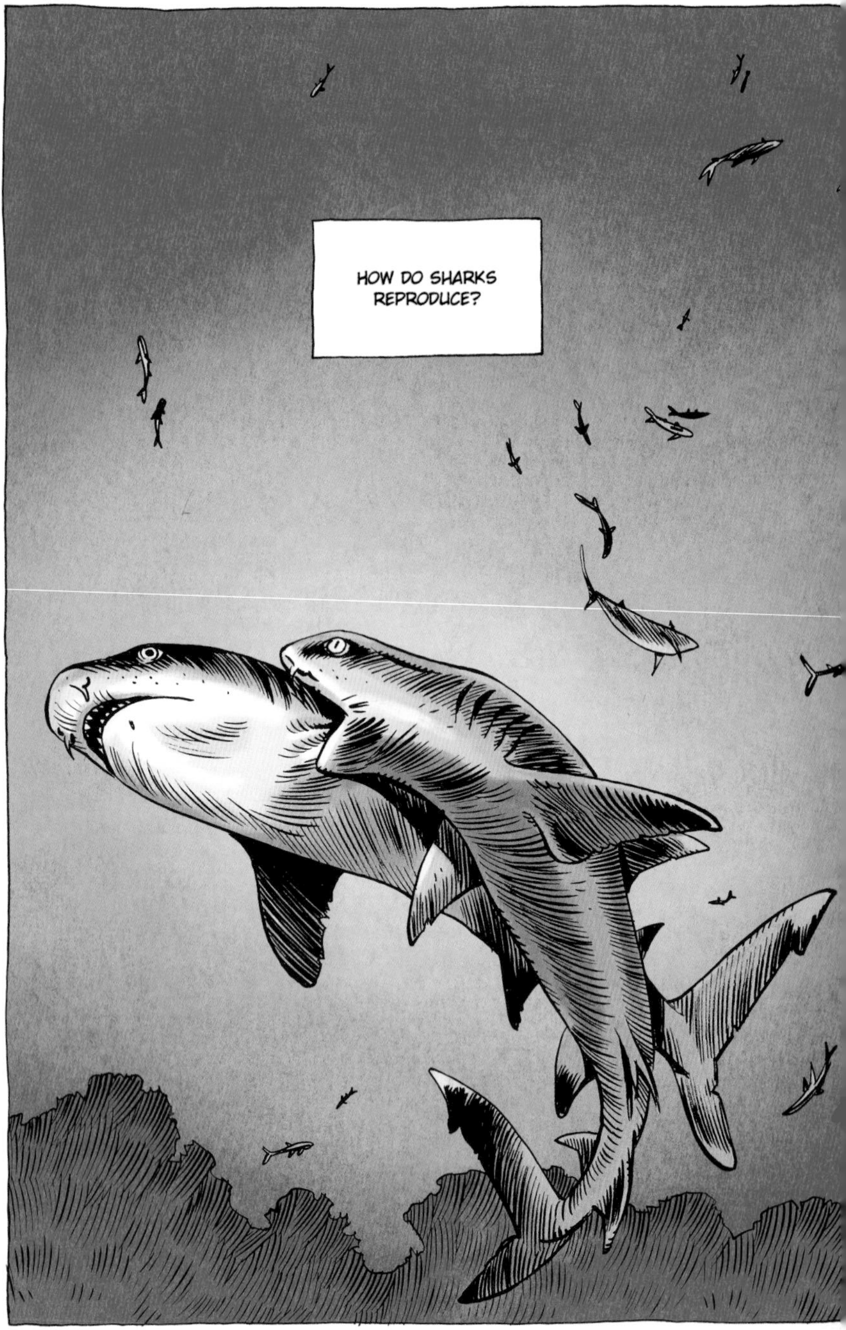
HOW DO SHARKS REPRODUCE?

AMONG SHARKS, MATING OCCURS BETWEEN ONE FEMALE AND ONE OR SEVERAL MALES.

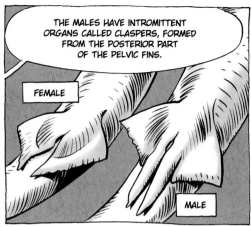

THE MALES HAVE INTROMITTENT ORGANS CALLED CLASPERS, FORMED FROM THE POSTERIOR PART OF THE PELVIC FINS.

FEMALE

MALE

AFTER A BRIEF COURTSHIP, THE MALE GRASPS THE FEMALE BY BITING HER, AND THEN INSERTS ONE OF ITS CLASPERS INTO HER CLOACA. FEMALES MAY SOMETIMES COME AWAY FROM THESE FIERCE FROLICS WITH BITE MARKS!

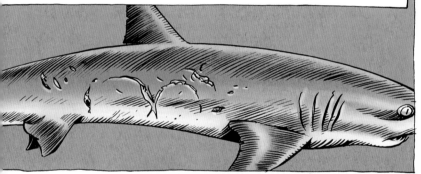

SHARKS DISPLAY THREE MAIN WAYS OF BEARING THEIR YOUNG.

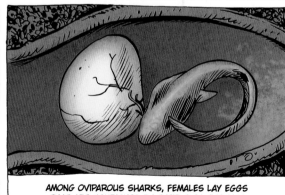

AMONG OVIPAROUS SHARKS, FEMALES LAY EGGS THAT ARE NOURISHED BY THEIR OWN VITELLINE RESERVE (EGG YOLK AND FLUIDS).

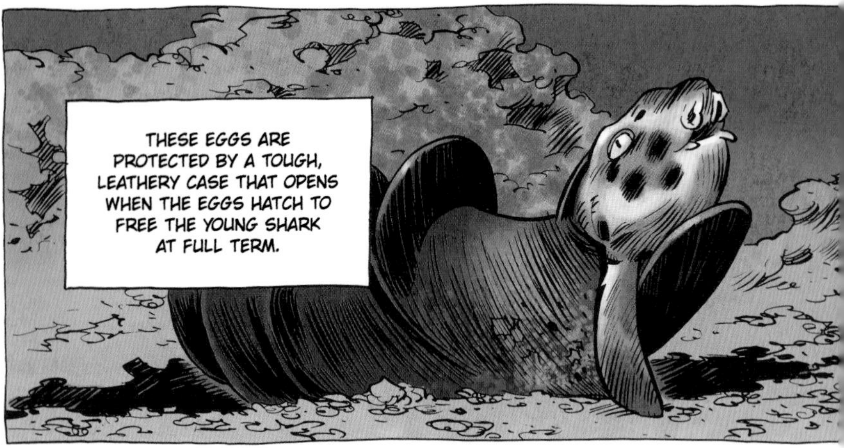
THESE EGGS ARE PROTECTED BY A TOUGH, LEATHERY CASE THAT OPENS WHEN THE EGGS HATCH TO FREE THE YOUNG SHARK AT FULL TERM.

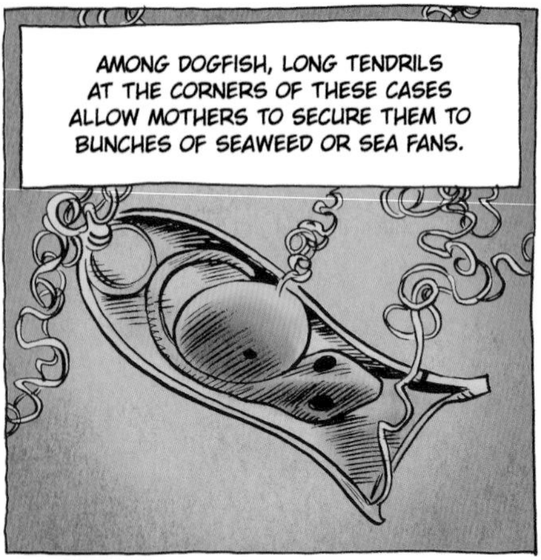
AMONG DOGFISH, LONG TENDRILS AT THE CORNERS OF THESE CASES ALLOW MOTHERS TO SECURE THEM TO BUNCHES OF SEAWEED OR SEA FANS.

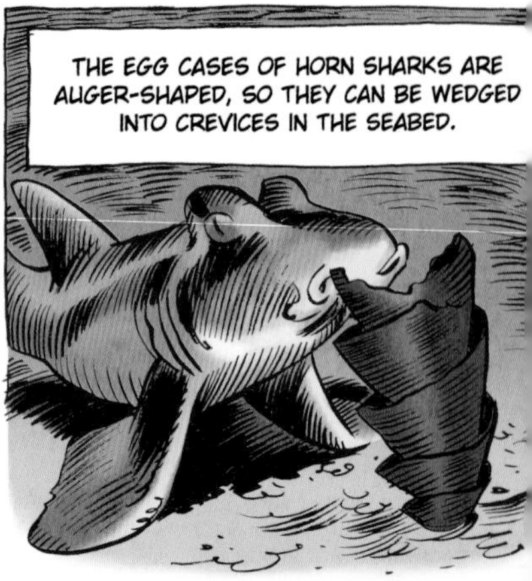
THE EGG CASES OF HORN SHARKS ARE AUGER-SHAPED, SO THEY CAN BE WEDGED INTO CREVICES IN THE SEABED.

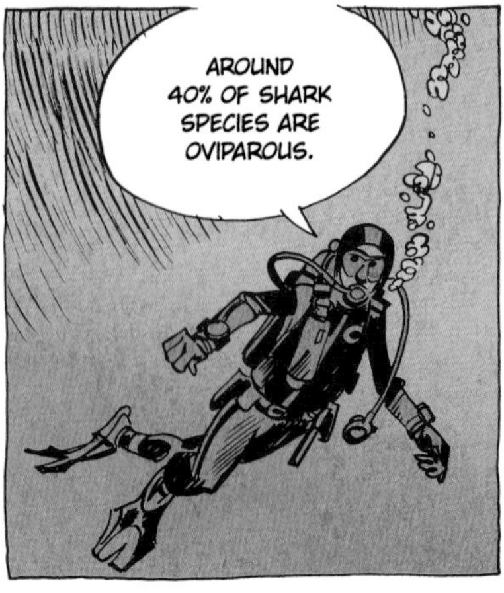
AROUND 40% OF SHARK SPECIES ARE OVIPAROUS.

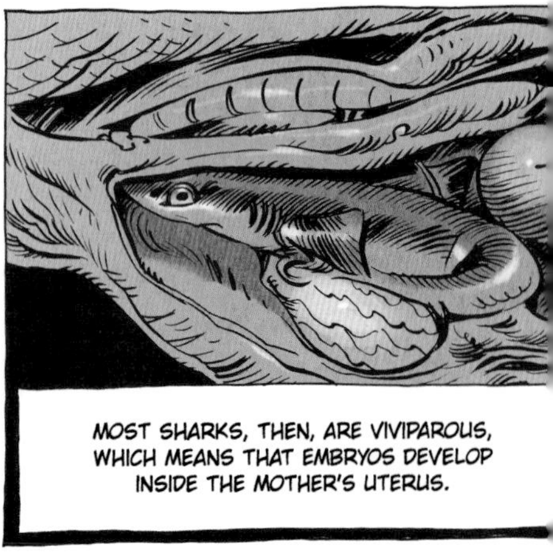
MOST SHARKS, THEN, ARE VIVIPAROUS, WHICH MEANS THAT EMBRYOS DEVELOP INSIDE THE MOTHER'S UTERUS.

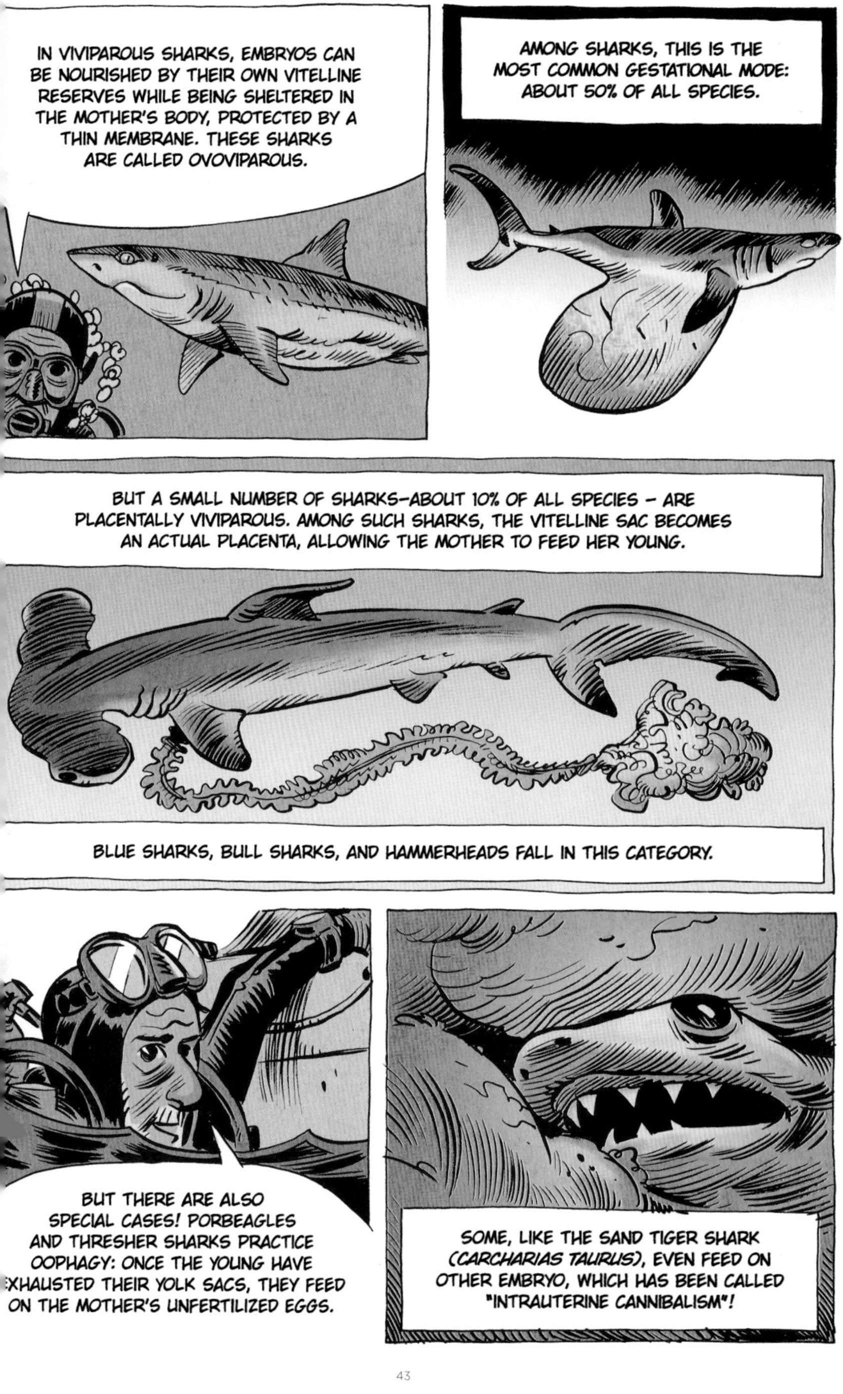

IN VIVIPAROUS SHARKS, EMBRYOS CAN BE NOURISHED BY THEIR OWN VITELLINE RESERVES WHILE BEING SHELTERED IN THE MOTHER'S BODY, PROTECTED BY A THIN MEMBRANE. THESE SHARKS ARE CALLED OVOVIPAROUS.
AMONG SHARKS, THIS IS THE MOST COMMON GESTATIONAL MODE: ABOUT 50% OF ALL SPECIES.
BUT A SMALL NUMBER OF SHARKS–ABOUT 10% OF ALL SPECIES – ARE PLACENTALLY VIVIPAROUS. AMONG SUCH SHARKS, THE VITELLINE SAC BECOMES AN ACTUAL PLACENTA, ALLOWING THE MOTHER TO FEED HER YOUNG.
BLUE SHARKS, BULL SHARKS, AND HAMMERHEADS FALL IN THIS CATEGORY.
BUT THERE ARE ALSO SPECIAL CASES! PORBEAGLES AND THRESHER SHARKS PRACTICE OOPHAGY: ONCE THE YOUNG HAVE EXHAUSTED THEIR YOLK SACS, THEY FEED ON THE MOTHER'S UNFERTILIZED EGGS.
SOME, LIKE THE SAND TIGER SHARK (*CARCHARIAS TAURUS*), EVEN FEED ON OTHER EMBRYO, WHICH HAS BEEN CALLED "INTRAUTERINE CANNIBALISM"!

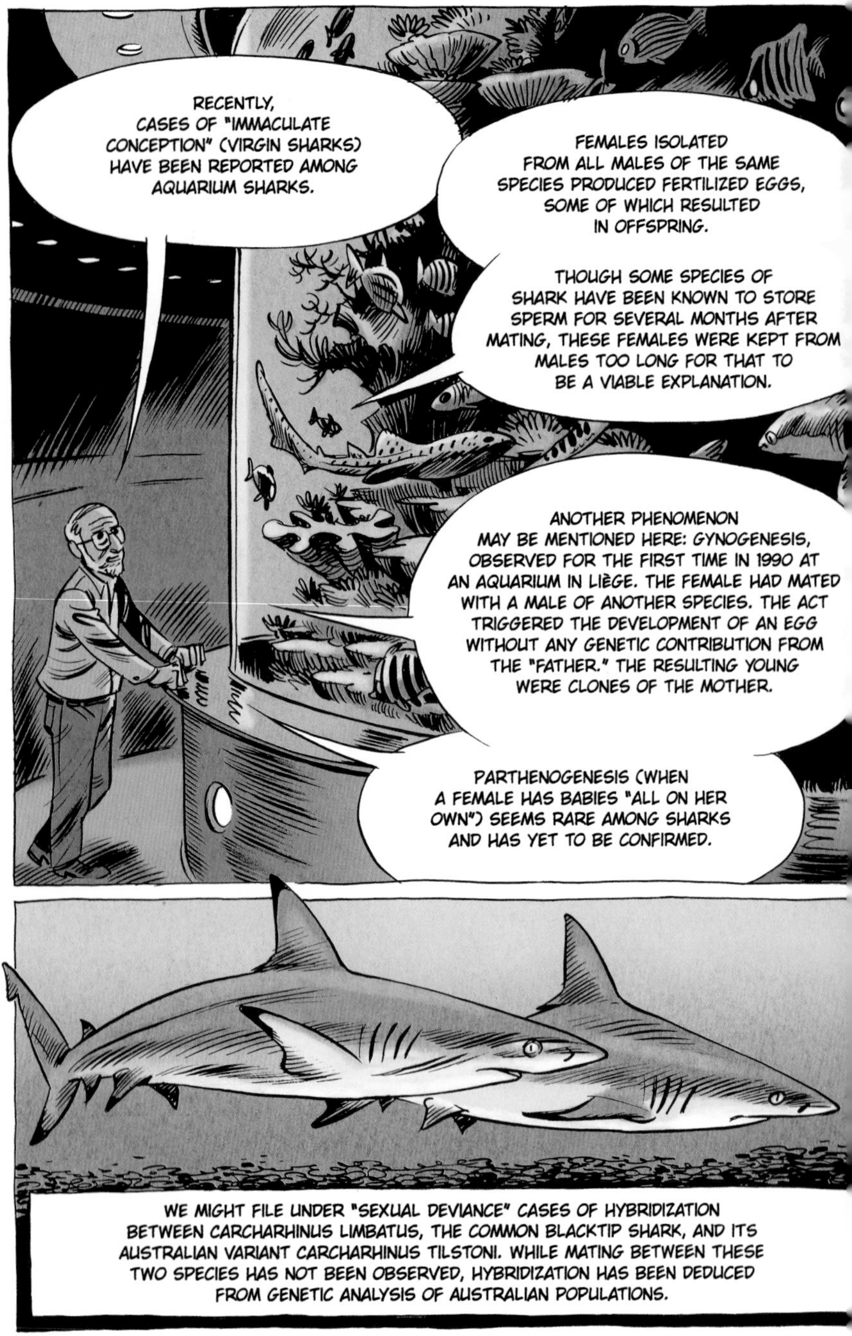
RECENTLY, CASES OF "IMMACULATE CONCEPTION" (VIRGIN SHARKS) HAVE BEEN REPORTED AMONG AQUARIUM SHARKS.
FEMALES ISOLATED FROM ALL MALES OF THE SAME SPECIES PRODUCED FERTILIZED EGGS, SOME OF WHICH RESULTED IN OFFSPRING.
THOUGH SOME SPECIES OF SHARK HAVE BEEN KNOWN TO STORE SPERM FOR SEVERAL MONTHS AFTER MATING, THESE FEMALES WERE KEPT FROM MALES TOO LONG FOR THAT TO BE A VIABLE EXPLANATION.
ANOTHER PHENOMENON MAY BE MENTIONED HERE: GYNOGENESIS, OBSERVED FOR THE FIRST TIME IN 1990 AT AN AQUARIUM IN LIÈGE. THE FEMALE HAD MATED WITH A MALE OF ANOTHER SPECIES. THE ACT TRIGGERED THE DEVELOPMENT OF AN EGG WITHOUT ANY GENETIC CONTRIBUTION FROM THE "FATHER." THE RESULTING YOUNG WERE CLONES OF THE MOTHER.
PARTHENOGENESIS (WHEN A FEMALE HAS BABIES "ALL ON HER OWN") SEEMS RARE AMONG SHARKS AND HAS YET TO BE CONFIRMED.
WE MIGHT FILE UNDER "SEXUAL DEVIANCE" CASES OF HYBRIDIZATION BETWEEN CARCHARHINUS LIMBATUS, THE COMMON BLACKTIP SHARK, AND ITS AUSTRALIAN VARIANT CARCHARHINUS TILSTONI. WHILE MATING BETWEEN THESE TWO SPECIES HAS NOT BEEN OBSERVED, HYBRIDIZATION HAS BEEN DEDUCED FROM GENETIC ANALYSIS OF AUSTRALIAN POPULATIONS.

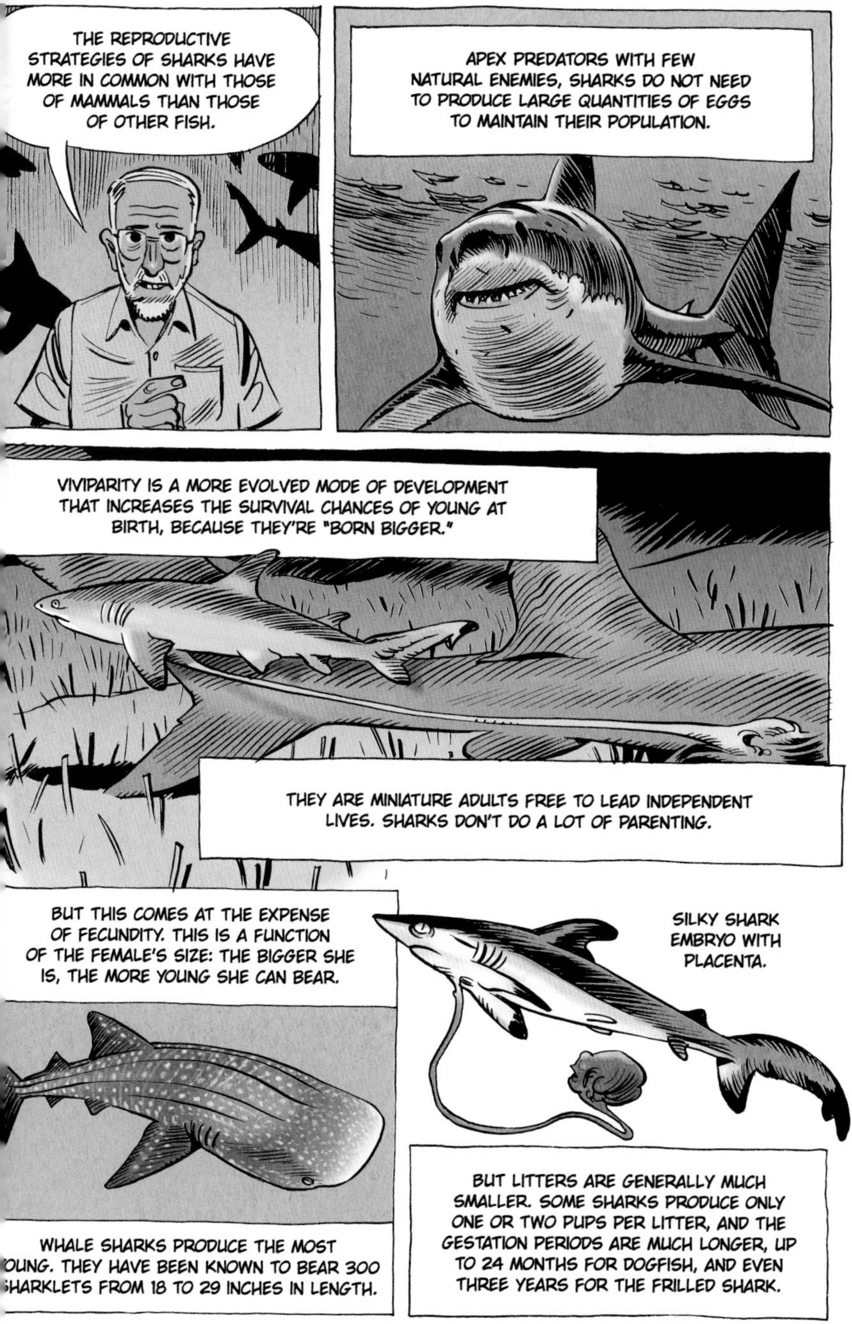

THE REPRODUCTIVE STRATEGIES OF SHARKS HAVE MORE IN COMMON WITH THOSE OF MAMMALS THAN THOSE OF OTHER FISH.

APEX PREDATORS WITH FEW NATURAL ENEMIES, SHARKS DO NOT NEED TO PRODUCE LARGE QUANTITIES OF EGGS TO MAINTAIN THEIR POPULATION.

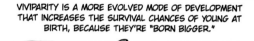

VIVIPARITY IS A MORE EVOLVED MODE OF DEVELOPMENT THAT INCREASES THE SURVIVAL CHANCES OF YOUNG AT BIRTH, BECAUSE THEY'RE "BORN BIGGER."

THEY ARE MINIATURE ADULTS FREE TO LEAD INDEPENDENT LIVES. SHARKS DON'T DO A LOT OF PARENTING.

BUT THIS COMES AT THE EXPENSE OF FECUNDITY. THIS IS A FUNCTION OF THE FEMALE'S SIZE: THE BIGGER SHE IS, THE MORE YOUNG SHE CAN BEAR.

SILKY SHARK EMBRYO WITH PLACENTA.

WHALE SHARKS PRODUCE THE MOST YOUNG. THEY HAVE BEEN KNOWN TO BEAR 300 SHARKLETS FROM 18 TO 29 INCHES IN LENGTH.

BUT LITTERS ARE GENERALLY MUCH SMALLER. SOME SHARKS PRODUCE ONLY ONE OR TWO PUPS PER LITTER, AND THE GESTATION PERIODS ARE MUCH LONGER, UP TO 24 MONTHS FOR DOGFISH, AND EVEN THREE YEARS FOR THE FRILLED SHARK.

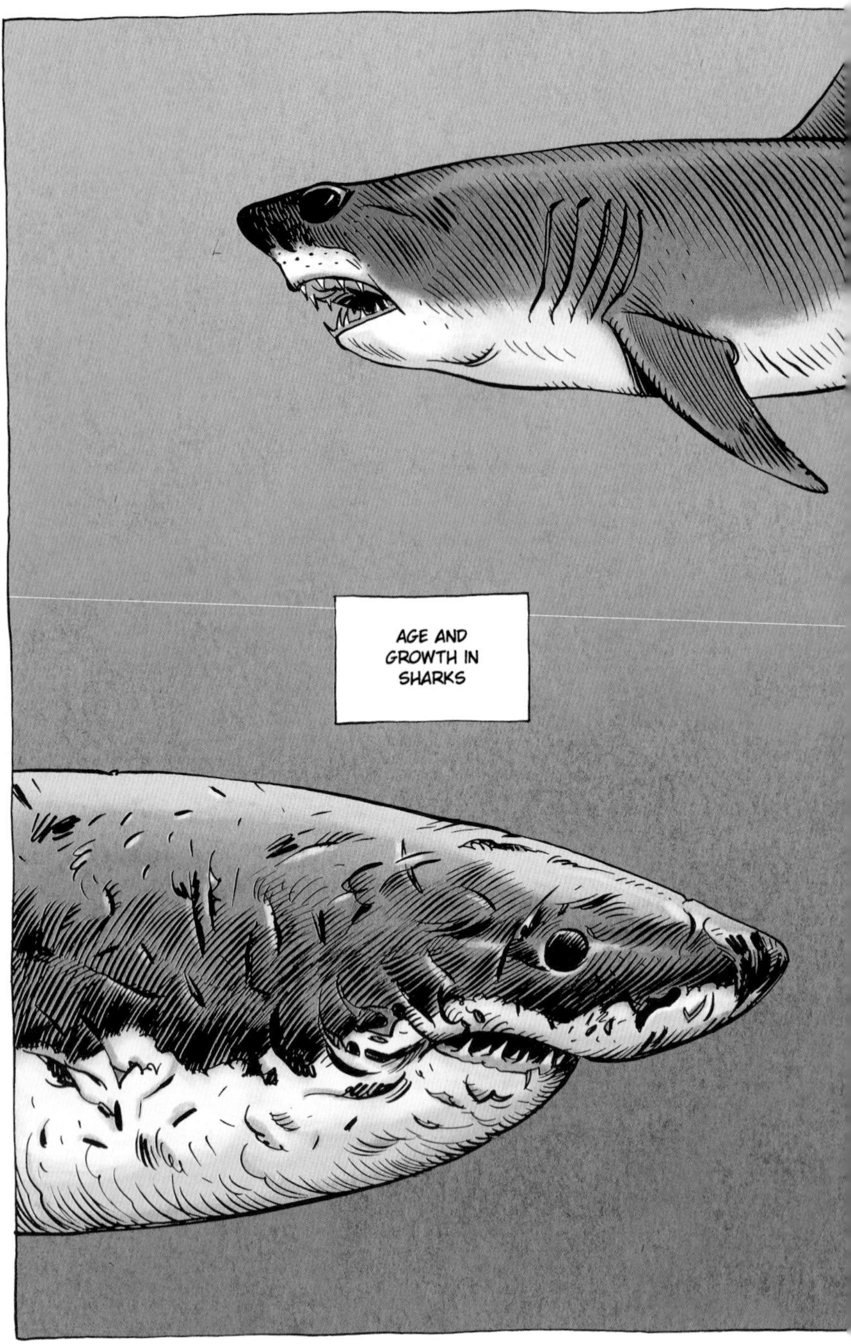
AGE AND GROWTH IN SHARKS

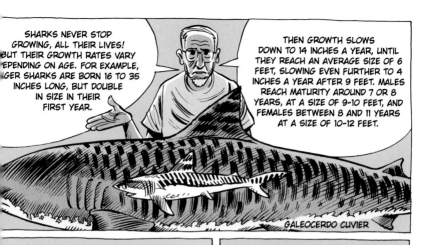

SHARKS NEVER STOP GROWING, ALL THEIR LIVES! BUT THEIR GROWTH RATES VARY DEPENDING ON AGE. FOR EXAMPLE, TIGER SHARKS ARE BORN 16 TO 35 INCHES LONG, BUT DOUBLE IN SIZE IN THEIR FIRST YEAR.

THEN GROWTH SLOWS DOWN TO 14 INCHES A YEAR, UNTIL THEY REACH AN AVERAGE SIZE OF 6 FEET, SLOWING EVEN FURTHER TO 4 INCHES A YEAR AFTER 9 FEET. MALES REACH MATURITY AROUND 7 OR 8 YEARS, AT A SIZE OF 9-10 FEET, AND FEMALES BETWEEN 8 AND 11 YEARS AT A SIZE OF 10-12 FEET.

GALEOCERDO CUVIER

THE SPINY DOGFISH IS BORN AROUND 7-12 INCHES AND REACHES SEXUAL MATURITY AFTER 10-25 YEARS (20-40 INCHES).

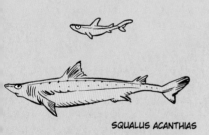

SQUALUS ACANTHIAS

THE SMALL-SPOTTED CATSHARK GOES FROM 4 INCHES AT BIRTH TO 16-17 INCHES AT MATURITY IN 3-5 YEARS.

SCYLIORHINUS CANICULA

A SHARK BEING MEASURED FOR SIZE.

ESTIMATING A SHARK'S AGE ISN'T EASY: UNLIKE BONY FISH, THEY LACK SCALES TO RECORD GROWTH IN THE FORM OF RINGS, WHICH WE CAN COUNT TO CALCULATE THE AGE (JUST AS WITH TREES).

IF IT'S RINGS YOU'RE AFTER, YOU HAVE TO EXAMINE THE VERTEBRAE, OR DORSAL SPINES IF THERE ARE ANY.

THESE RINGS ARE ALTERNATELY LIGHT AND DARK, BUT THEY ARE OFTEN LESS PRONOUNCED IN TROPICAL SPECIES, BECAUSE THERE'S LESS SEASONAL VARIATION IN THEIR DIET.

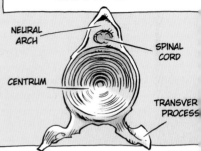

NEURAL ARCH

SPINAL CORD

CENTRUM

TRANSVER PROCESS

IN ORDER TO ESTIMATE AGE BY COUNTING RINGS, ANOTHER THING MUST BE VERIFIED: THAT THERE ARE TWO GROWTH RINGS PER YEAR (ONE LIGHT AND ONE DARK).

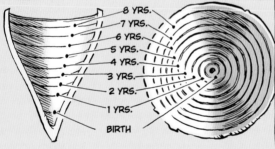

8 YRS.
7 YRS.
6 YRS.
5 YRS.
4 YRS.
3 YRS.
2 YRS.
1 YRS.

BIRTH

THAT'S BEEN GATHERED IS PLUGGED INTO AN EQUATION AND TURNED INTO A GRAPH.

VON BERTALANFFY'S MODEL REMAINS THE MOST CURRENT OF AN ORGANISM'S GROWTH OVER TIME, WITH RAPID GROWTH IN YOUTH AND A CLEAR SLOWING DOWN AFTER SEXUAL MATURITY.

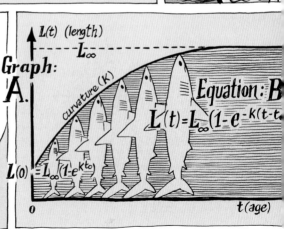

Graph: A.

$L(t)$ (length)

L_∞

curvature (k)

Equation: B

$L(t) = L_\infty (1 - e^{-k(t-t_0)})$

$L(0) = L_\infty (1 - e^{kt_0})$

0

t (age)

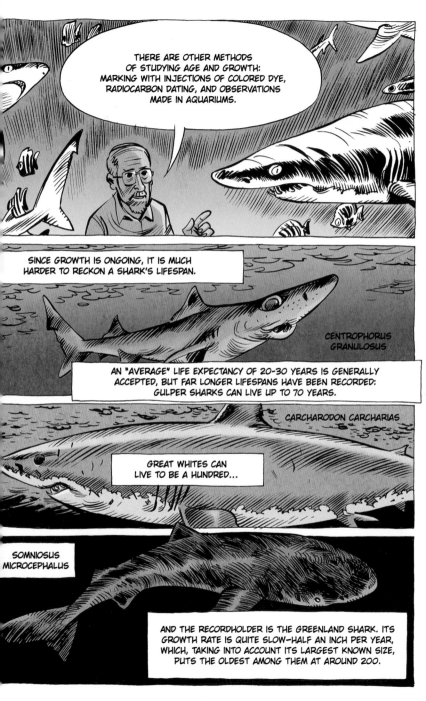

THERE ARE OTHER METHODS OF STUDYING AGE AND GROWTH: MARKING WITH INJECTIONS OF COLORED DYE, RADIOCARBON DATING, AND OBSERVATIONS MADE IN AQUARIUMS.

SINCE GROWTH IS ONGOING, IT IS MUCH HARDER TO RECKON A SHARK'S LIFESPAN.

CENTROPHORUS GRANULOSUS

AN "AVERAGE" LIFE EXPECTANCY OF 20-30 YEARS IS GENERALLY ACCEPTED, BUT FAR LONGER LIFESPANS HAVE BEEN RECORDED: GULPER SHARKS CAN LIVE UP TO 70 YEARS.

CARCHARODON CARCHARIAS

GREAT WHITES CAN LIVE TO BE A HUNDRED...

SOMNIOSUS MICROCEPHALUS

AND THE RECORDHOLDER IS THE GREENLAND SHARK. ITS GROWTH RATE IS QUITE SLOW—HALF AN INCH PER YEAR, WHICH, TAKING INTO ACCOUNT ITS LARGEST KNOWN SIZE, PUTS THE OLDEST AMONG THEM AT AROUND 200.

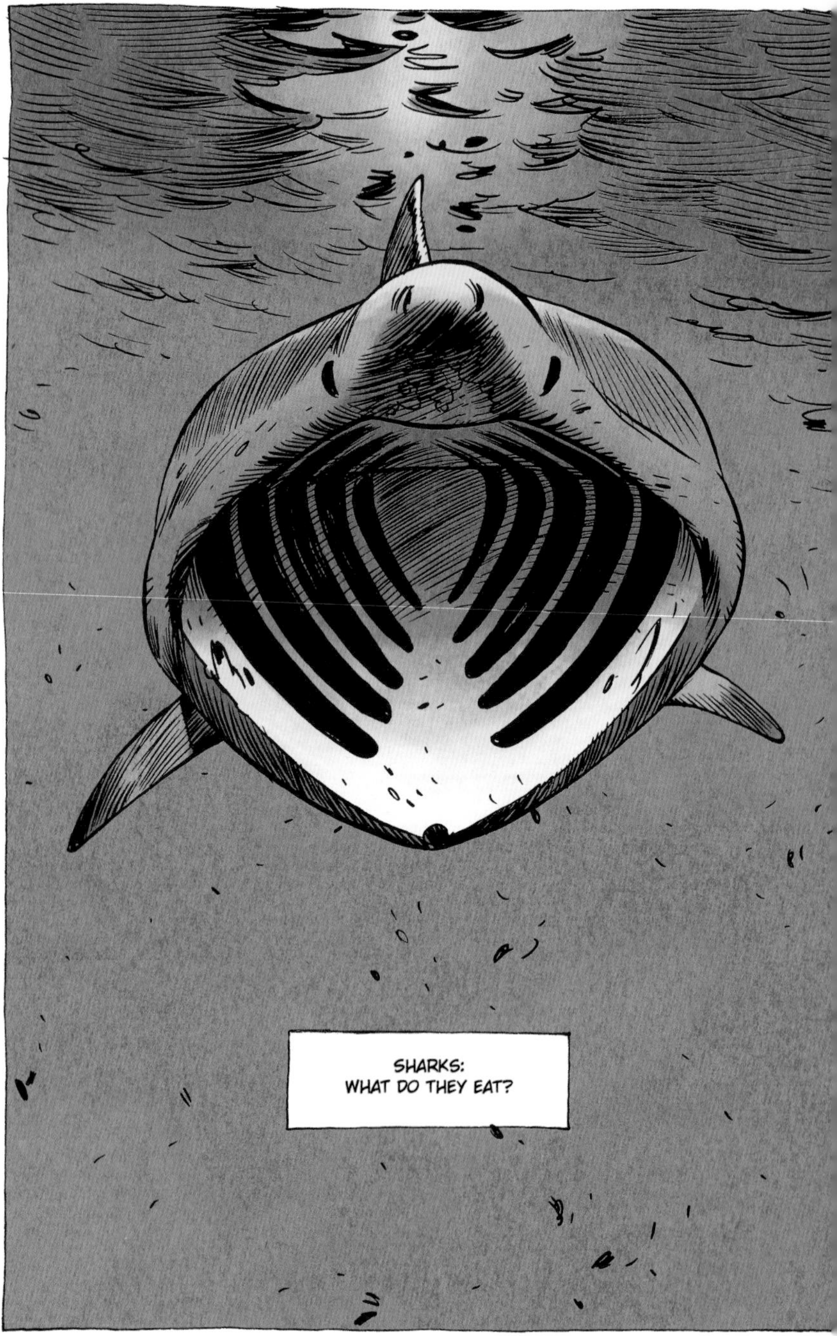
SHARKS:
WHAT DO THEY EAT?

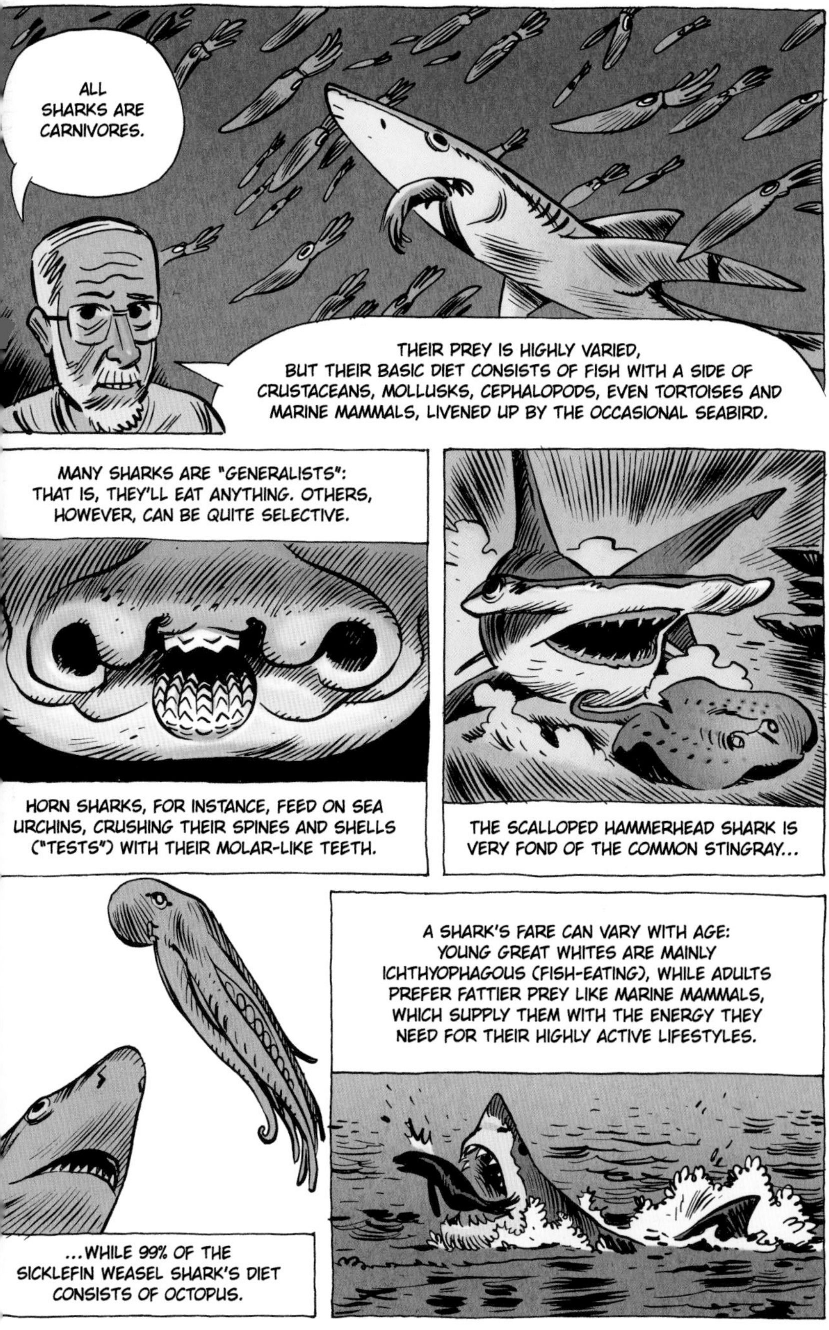
ALL SHARKS ARE CARNIVORES.
THEIR PREY IS HIGHLY VARIED, BUT THEIR BASIC DIET CONSISTS OF FISH WITH A SIDE OF CRUSTACEANS, MOLLUSKS, CEPHALOPODS, EVEN TORTOISES AND MARINE MAMMALS, LIVENED UP BY THE OCCASIONAL SEABIRD.
MANY SHARKS ARE "GENERALISTS": THAT IS, THEY'LL EAT ANYTHING. OTHERS, HOWEVER, CAN BE QUITE SELECTIVE.
HORN SHARKS, FOR INSTANCE, FEED ON SEA URCHINS, CRUSHING THEIR SPINES AND SHELLS ("TESTS") WITH THEIR MOLAR-LIKE TEETH.
THE SCALLOPED HAMMERHEAD SHARK IS VERY FOND OF THE COMMON STINGRAY...
...WHILE 99% OF THE SICKLEFIN WEASEL SHARK'S DIET CONSISTS OF OCTOPUS.
A SHARK'S FARE CAN VARY WITH AGE: YOUNG GREAT WHITES ARE MAINLY ICHTHYOPHAGOUS (FISH-EATING), WHILE ADULTS PREFER FATTIER PREY LIKE MARINE MAMMALS, WHICH SUPPLY THEM WITH THE ENERGY THEY NEED FOR THEIR HIGHLY ACTIVE LIFESTYLES.

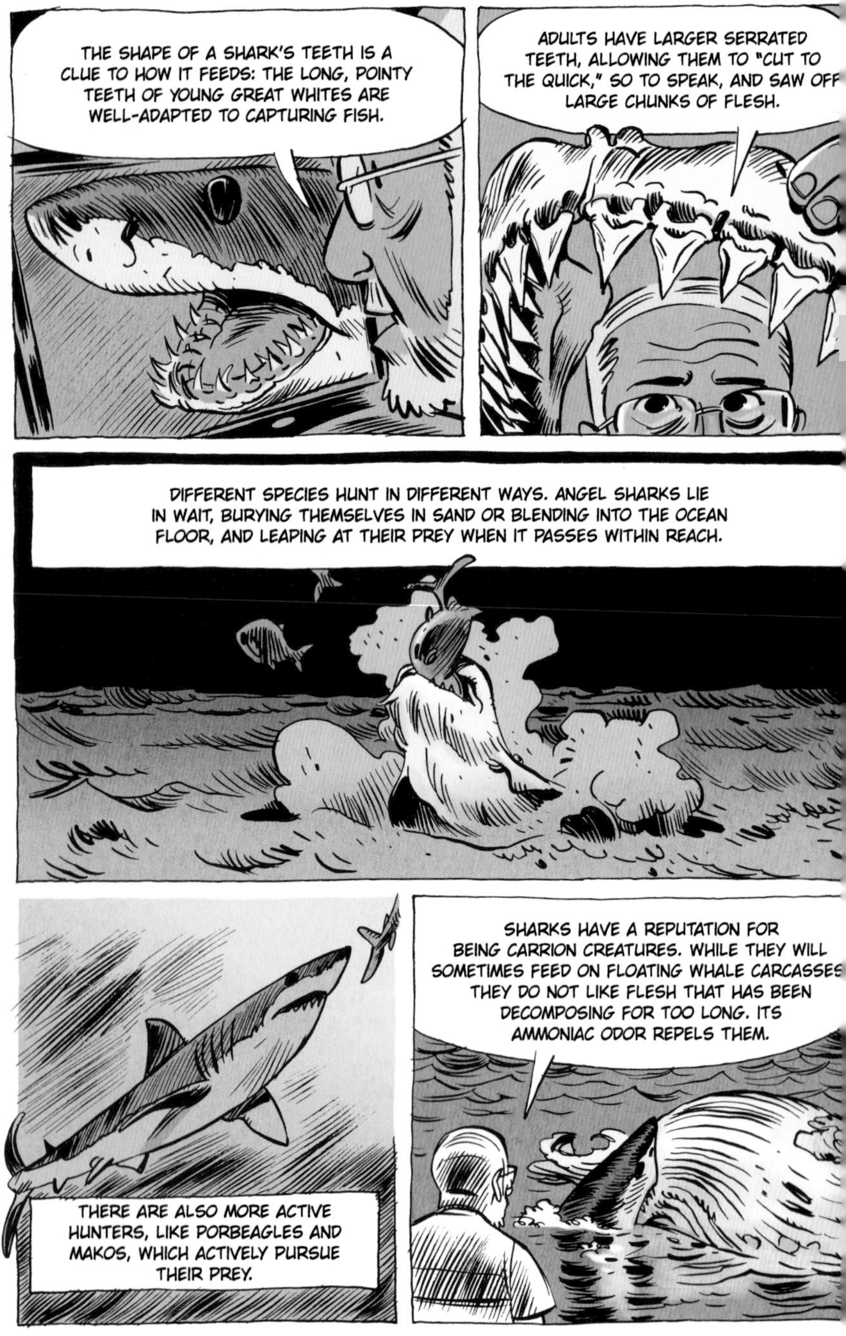
THE SHAPE OF A SHARK'S TEETH IS A CLUE TO HOW IT FEEDS: THE LONG, POINTY TEETH OF YOUNG GREAT WHITES ARE WELL-ADAPTED TO CAPTURING FISH.
ADULTS HAVE LARGER SERRATED TEETH, ALLOWING THEM TO "CUT TO THE QUICK," SO TO SPEAK, AND SAW OFF LARGE CHUNKS OF FLESH.
DIFFERENT SPECIES HUNT IN DIFFERENT WAYS. ANGEL SHARKS LIE IN WAIT, BURYING THEMSELVES IN SAND OR BLENDING INTO THE OCEAN FLOOR, AND LEAPING AT THEIR PREY WHEN IT PASSES WITHIN REACH.
THERE ARE ALSO MORE ACTIVE HUNTERS, LIKE PORBEAGLES AND MAKOS, WHICH ACTIVELY PURSUE THEIR PREY.
SHARKS HAVE A REPUTATION FOR BEING CARRION CREATURES. WHILE THEY WILL SOMETIMES FEED ON FLOATING WHALE CARCASSES THEY DO NOT LIKE FLESH THAT HAS BEEN DECOMPOSING FOR TOO LONG. ITS AMMONIAC ODOR REPELS THEM.

SOME BENTHIC SHARKS HAVE RATHER ORIGINAL METHODS OF PREDATION. THE GOBLIN SHARK (MITSUKURINA OWSTONI) IS ABLE TO "CATAPULT" ITS JAWS FORWARD TO SEIZE PREY. AT SUCH DEPTHS, PREY ARE RARE, AND NOT TO BE PASSED UP.

THE VIPER DOGFISH (TRIGONOGNATHUS KABEYAI) CAN PROTRUDE ITS JAW FORWARD AND "SKEWER" ITS PREY ON ITS LONG, NEEDLE-LIKE TEETH.

THRESHER SHARKS HAVE A RATHER UNIQUE APPROACH TO THE HUNT.

THEY FEED ON SMALL PELAGIC FISH THAT LIVE IN SHOALS. THESE SHARKS "THRESH" THE WATER WITH THEIR LONG TAILS, SWATTING AND STUNNING PREY BEFORE FEEDING.

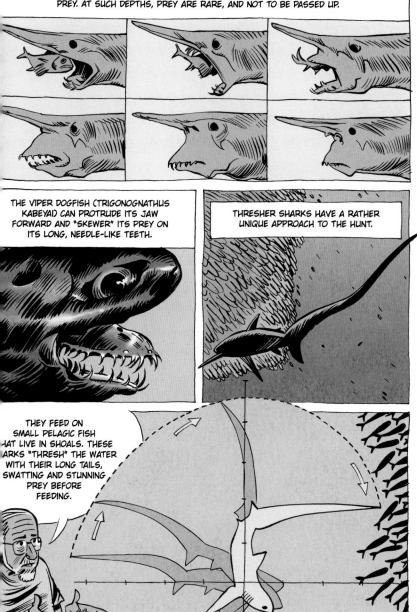

TIGER SHARKS AREN'T VERY PARTICULAR: IT'S ALL FOOD TO THEM, EVEN THE MOST ECLECTIC OBJECTS.

AT THE MUSEUM OF THE SEA ON GORÉE ISLAND, SENEGAL, IS A TOM-TOM THAT WAS FOUND IN A TIGER SHARK'S BELLY!

UPON SWALLOWING AN ITEM THAT THEY CAN'T DIGEST, SOME SHARKS ARE ABLE TO REGURGITATE IT BY TURNING THEIR STOMACHS INSIDE OUT.

SOMETIMES, SHARKS WILL EAT EACH OTHER, THE BIGGEST DEVOURING THE SMALLEST. CASES OF CANNIBALISM HAVE ALSO BEEN OBSERVED, ESPECIALLY RIGHT AFTER BIRTH: SOME FATHERS WON'T THINK TWICE ABOUT SNACKING ON THEIR YOUNG!

BUT THERE ARE EXCEPTIONS: PLANKTON FILTER-FEEDERS LIKE BASKING SHARKS, WHALE SHARKS, AND MEGAMOUTH SHARKS.

THESE THREE HAVE MASSIVE MOUTHS AND LARGE GILL ARCHES FOR FILTERING ENORMOUS QUANTITIES OF WATER AND RETAINING TINY ORGANISMS GATHERED IN THE MUCUS TO BE SWALLOWED.

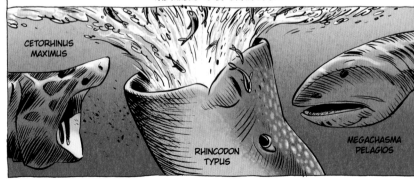

CETORHINUS MAXIMUS

RHINCODON TYPUS

MEGACHASMA PELAGIOS

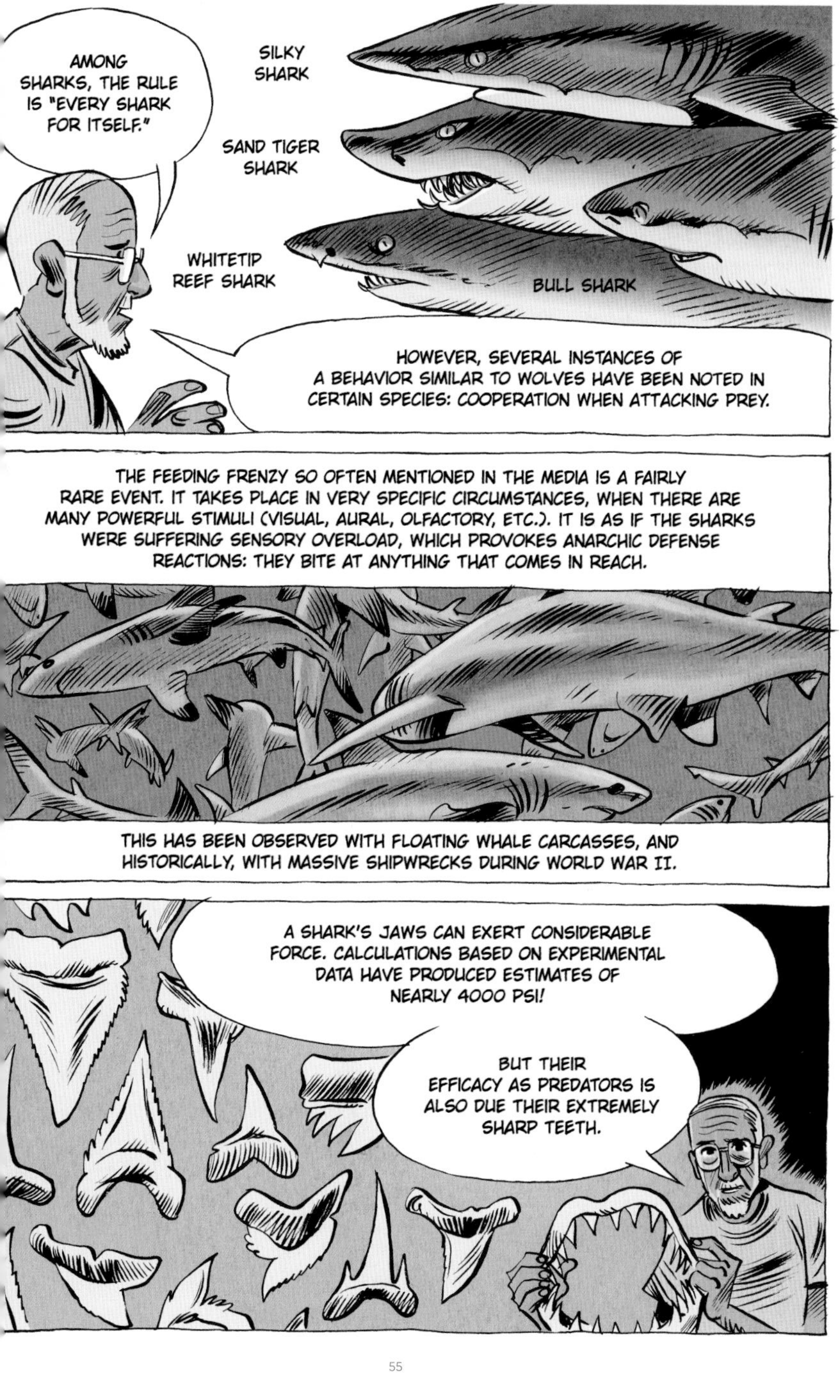
AMONG SHARKS, THE RULE IS "EVERY SHARK FOR ITSELF."
SILKY SHARK
SAND TIGER SHARK
WHITETIP REEF SHARK
BULL SHARK
HOWEVER, SEVERAL INSTANCES OF A BEHAVIOR SIMILAR TO WOLVES HAVE BEEN NOTED IN CERTAIN SPECIES: COOPERATION WHEN ATTACKING PREY.
THE FEEDING FRENZY SO OFTEN MENTIONED IN THE MEDIA IS A FAIRLY RARE EVENT. IT TAKES PLACE IN VERY SPECIFIC CIRCUMSTANCES, WHEN THERE ARE MANY POWERFUL STIMULI (VISUAL, AURAL, OLFACTORY, ETC.). IT IS AS IF THE SHARKS WERE SUFFERING SENSORY OVERLOAD, WHICH PROVOKES ANARCHIC DEFENSE REACTIONS: THEY BITE AT ANYTHING THAT COMES IN REACH.
THIS HAS BEEN OBSERVED WITH FLOATING WHALE CARCASSES, AND HISTORICALLY, WITH MASSIVE SHIPWRECKS DURING WORLD WAR II.
A SHARK'S JAWS CAN EXERT CONSIDERABLE FORCE. CALCULATIONS BASED ON EXPERIMENTAL DATA HAVE PRODUCED ESTIMATES OF NEARLY 4000 PSI!
BUT THEIR EFFICACY AS PREDATORS IS ALSO DUE THEIR EXTREMELY SHARP TEETH.

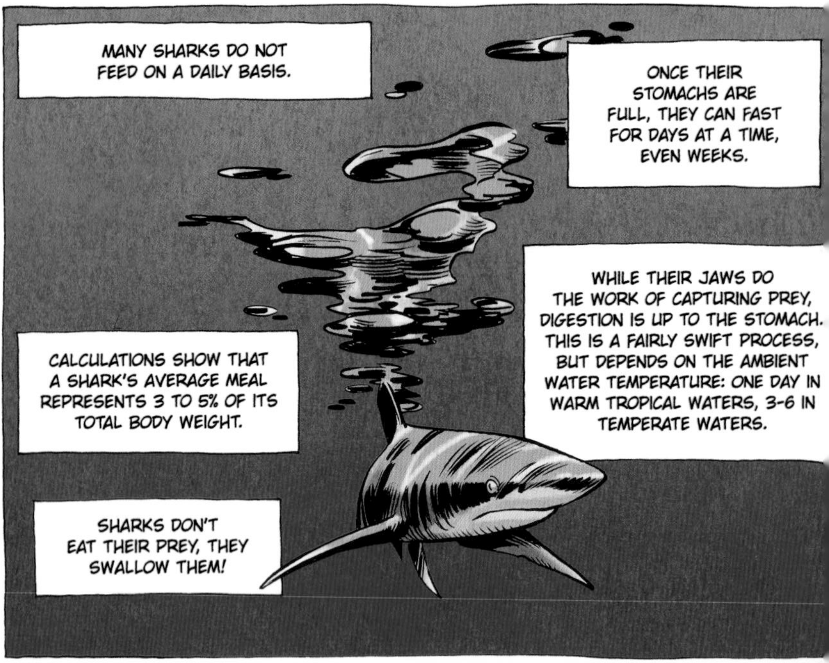
MANY SHARKS DO NOT FEED ON A DAILY BASIS.
ONCE THEIR STOMACHS ARE FULL, THEY CAN FAST FOR DAYS AT A TIME, EVEN WEEKS.
WHILE THEIR JAWS DO THE WORK OF CAPTURING PREY, DIGESTION IS UP TO THE STOMACH. THIS IS A FAIRLY SWIFT PROCESS, BUT DEPENDS ON THE AMBIENT WATER TEMPERATURE: ONE DAY IN WARM TROPICAL WATERS, 3-6 IN TEMPERATE WATERS.
CALCULATIONS SHOW THAT A SHARK'S AVERAGE MEAL REPRESENTS 3 TO 5% OF ITS TOTAL BODY WEIGHT.
SHARKS DON'T EAT THEIR PREY, THEY SWALLOW THEM!

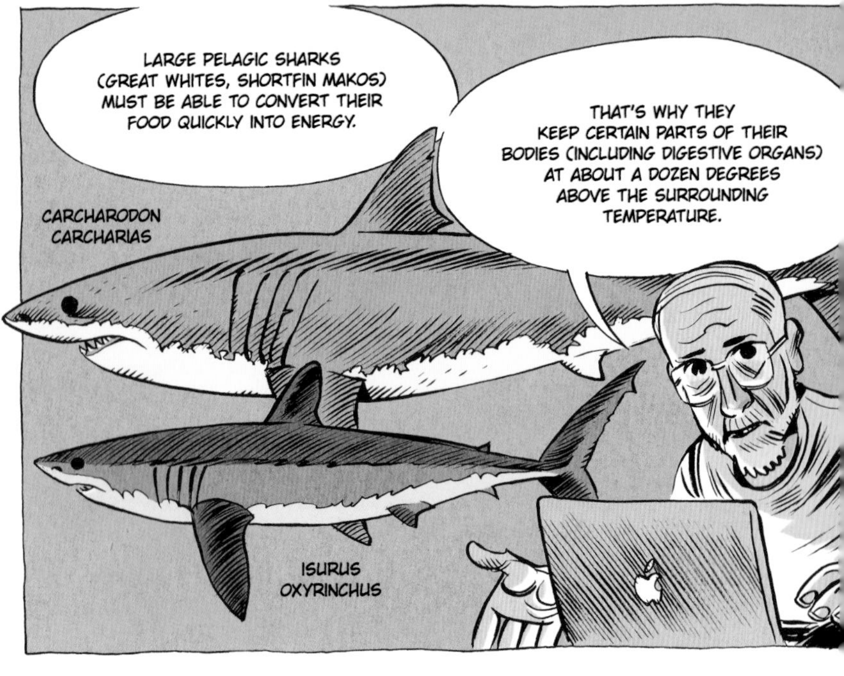
LARGE PELAGIC SHARKS (GREAT WHITES, SHORTFIN MAKOS) MUST BE ABLE TO CONVERT THEIR FOOD QUICKLY INTO ENERGY.
THAT'S WHY THEY KEEP CERTAIN PARTS OF THEIR BODIES (INCLUDING DIGESTIVE ORGANS) AT ABOUT A DOZEN DEGREES ABOVE THE SURROUNDING TEMPERATURE.
CARCHARODON CARCHARIAS
ISURUS OXYRINCHUS

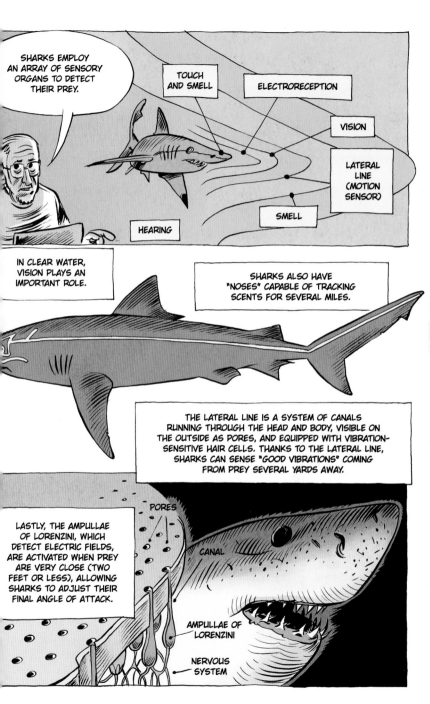

SHARKS EMPLOY AN ARRAY OF SENSORY ORGANS TO DETECT THEIR PREY.

TOUCH AND SMELL

ELECTRORECEPTION

VISION

LATERAL LINE (MOTION SENSOR)

SMELL

HEARING

IN CLEAR WATER, VISION PLAYS AN IMPORTANT ROLE.

SHARKS ALSO HAVE "NOSES" CAPABLE OF TRACKING SCENTS FOR SEVERAL MILES.

THE LATERAL LINE IS A SYSTEM OF CANALS RUNNING THROUGH THE HEAD AND BODY, VISIBLE ON THE OUTSIDE AS PORES, AND EQUIPPED WITH VIBRATION-SENSITIVE HAIR CELLS. THANKS TO THE LATERAL LINE, SHARKS CAN SENSE "GOOD VIBRATIONS" COMING FROM PREY SEVERAL YARDS AWAY.

PORES

LASTLY, THE AMPULLAE OF LORENZINI, WHICH DETECT ELECTRIC FIELDS, ARE ACTIVATED WHEN PREY ARE VERY CLOSE (TWO FEET OR LESS), ALLOWING SHARKS TO ADJUST THEIR FINAL ANGLE OF ATTACK.

CANAL

AMPULLAE OF LORENZINI

NERVOUS SYSTEM

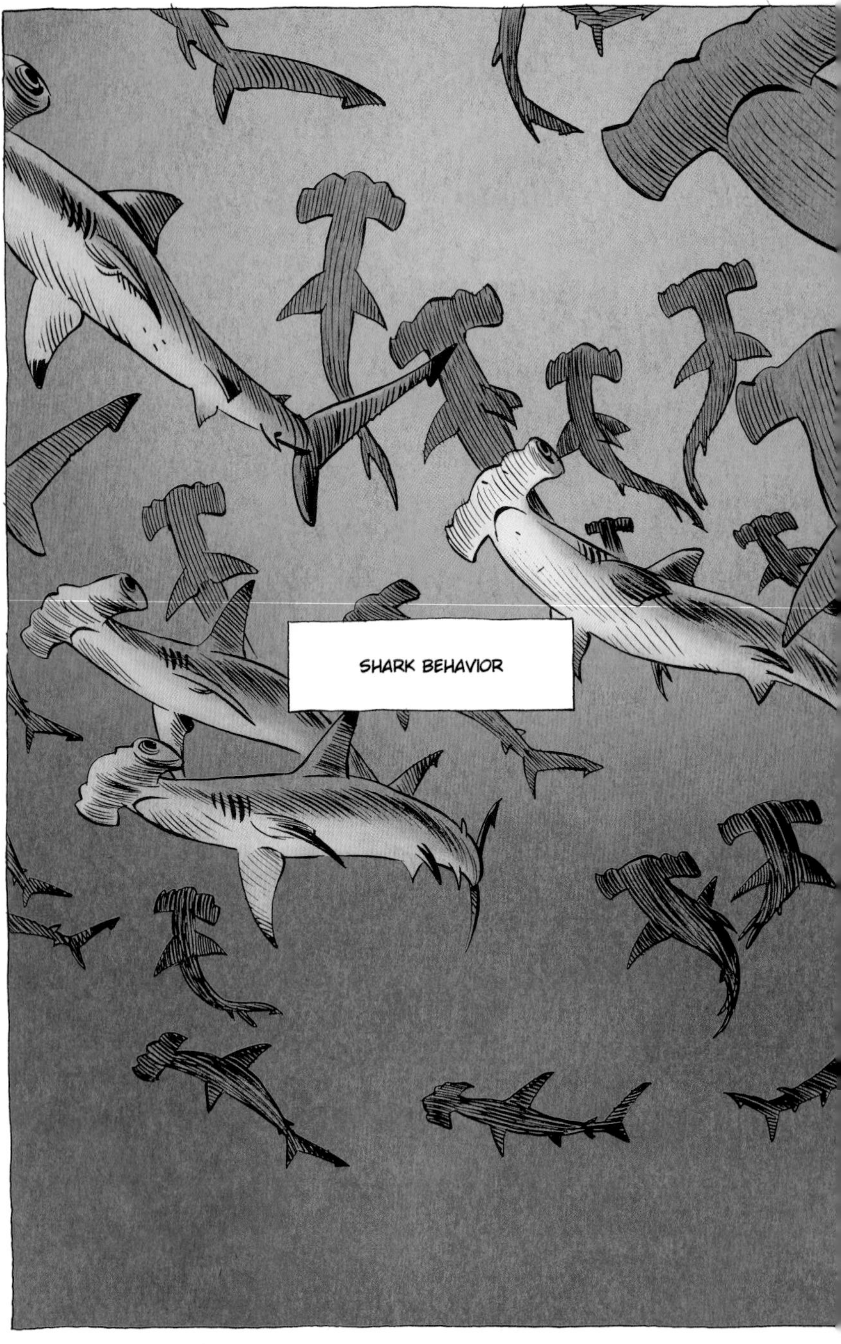
SHARK BEHAVIOR

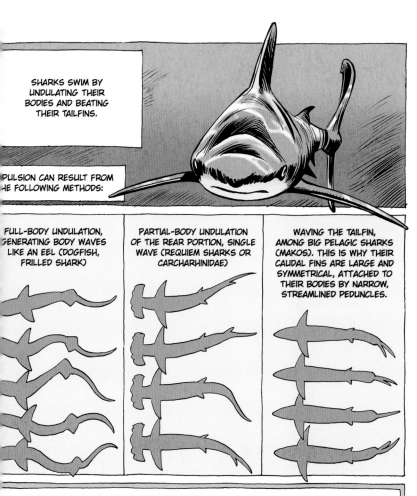

SHARKS SWIM BY UNDULATING THEIR BODIES AND BEATING THEIR TAILFINS.

...PULSION CAN RESULT FROM ...HE FOLLOWING METHODS:

FULL-BODY UNDULATION, ...GENERATING BODY WAVES LIKE AN EEL (DOGFISH, FRILLED SHARK)

PARTIAL-BODY UNDULATION OF THE REAR PORTION, SINGLE WAVE (REQUIEM SHARKS OR CARCHARHINIDAE)

WAVING THE TAILFIN, AMONG BIG PELAGIC SHARKS (MAKOS). THIS IS WHY THEIR CAUDAL FINS ARE LARGE AND SYMMETRICAL, ATTACHED TO THEIR BODIES BY NARROW, STREAMLINED PEDUNCLES.

SHARKS WHO ARE "GOOD SWIMMERS" HAVE HYDRODYNAMIC SHAPES THAT FACILITATE LOCOMOTION. TAIL SHAPE ALSO PLAYS ITS PART. GENERALLY, TAILS ARE HETEROCERCAL: THE DORSAL PORTION IS NOTICEABLY LARGER THAN THE VENTRAL PORTION, PARTIALLY COMPENSATING FOR SHARKS' NEGATIVE BUOYANCY. DERMAL DENTICLES ALSO CONTRIBUTE, REDUCING TURBULENCE ALONG THE BODY.

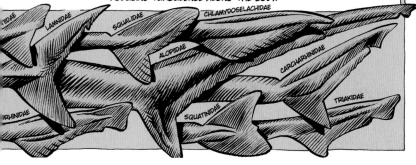

...IIDAE
LAMNIDAE
SQUALIDAE
CHLAMYDOSELACHIDAE
ALOPIIDAE
CARCHARHINIDAE
...RHINIDAE
SQUATINIDAE
TRIAKIDAE

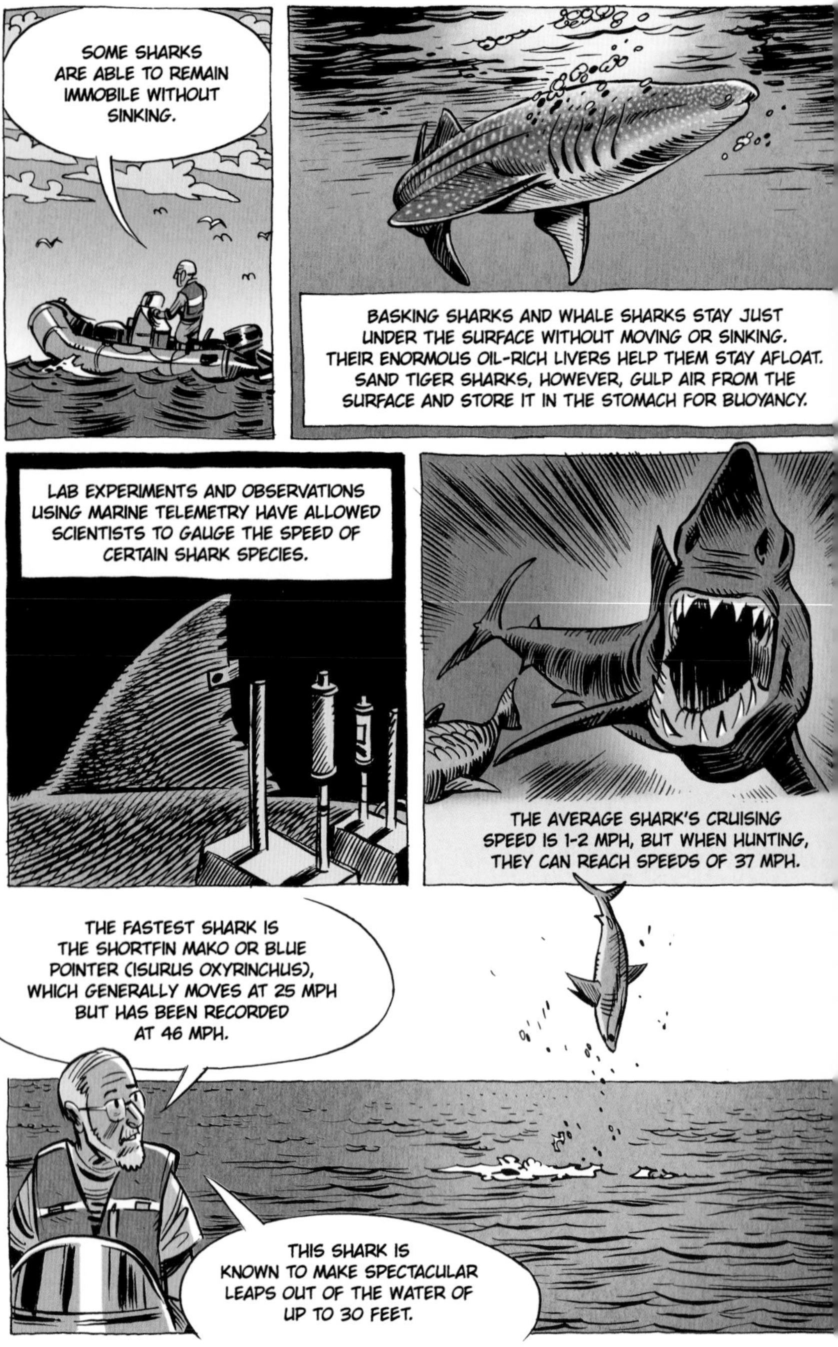
SOME SHARKS ARE ABLE TO REMAIN IMMOBILE WITHOUT SINKING.
BASKING SHARKS AND WHALE SHARKS STAY JUST UNDER THE SURFACE WITHOUT MOVING OR SINKING. THEIR ENORMOUS OIL-RICH LIVERS HELP THEM STAY AFLOAT. SAND TIGER SHARKS, HOWEVER, GULP AIR FROM THE SURFACE AND STORE IT IN THE STOMACH FOR BUOYANCY.
LAB EXPERIMENTS AND OBSERVATIONS USING MARINE TELEMETRY HAVE ALLOWED SCIENTISTS TO GAUGE THE SPEED OF CERTAIN SHARK SPECIES.
THE AVERAGE SHARK'S CRUISING SPEED IS 1-2 MPH, BUT WHEN HUNTING, THEY CAN REACH SPEEDS OF 37 MPH.
THE FASTEST SHARK IS THE SHORTFIN MAKO OR BLUE POINTER (ISURUS OXYRINCHUS), WHICH GENERALLY MOVES AT 25 MPH BUT HAS BEEN RECORDED AT 46 MPH.
THIS SHARK IS KNOWN TO MAKE SPECTACULAR LEAPS OUT OF THE WATER OF UP TO 30 FEET.

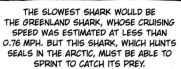

THE SLOWEST SHARK WOULD BE THE GREENLAND SHARK, WHOSE CRUISING SPEED WAS ESTIMATED AT LESS THAN 0.76 MPH. BUT THIS SHARK, WHICH HUNTS SEALS IN THE ARCTIC, MUST BE ABLE TO SPRINT TO CATCH ITS PREY.

PLANKTON FILTER-FEEDERS HAVE A CRUISING SPEED OF 3 MPH. FOR COMPARISON, OLYMPIC SWIMMERS CAN REACH SPEEDS OF 5 MPH, BUT ONLY FOR A FEW DOZEN SECONDS.

FOR SOME SHARKS, SWIMMING IS REQUIRED FOR BREATHING. BUT ARE THEY DOOMED TO BE IN CONSTANT MOTION?

DO THEY NEVER SLEEP?

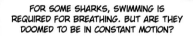

HOW SHARKS SLEEP REMAINS A MYSTERY.

THERE IS EVIDENCE AMONG BENTHIC SPECIES, WHICH LIVE IN THE DEPTHS, OF PERIODS OF REST. BUT WHAT ABOUT THE BIG PELAGIC SHARKS? DO THEY TAKE 2- OR 3-SECOND MICRO-NAPS, LIKE DOLPHINS, DURING WHICH ONLY ONE HEMISPHERE OF THEIR BRAIN IS FUNCTIONING? DO THEY SWIM WHILE ASLEEP?

POSSIBLY. THE NERVE CENTERS FOR LOCOMOTION ARE LOCATED IN THE MEDULLA OBLONGATA. THEY COULD CONCEIVABLY CONTINUE SWIMMING WHILE THEIR BRAINS ARE ASLEEP.

ADVANCES IN TELEMETRY MAY SOON BRING US THE ANSWER.

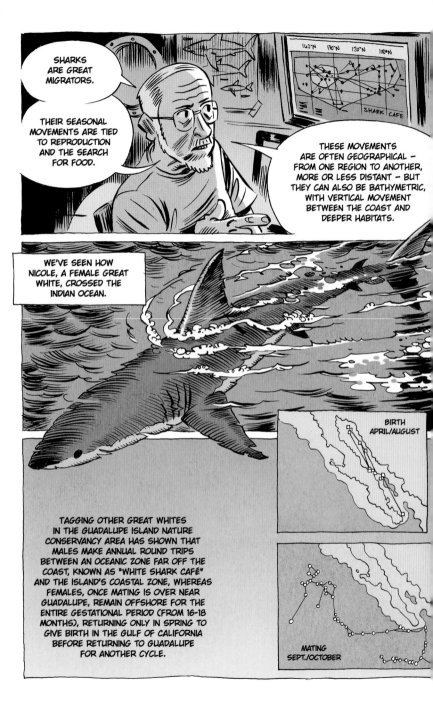

SHARKS ARE GREAT MIGRATORS.

THEIR SEASONAL MOVEMENTS ARE TIED TO REPRODUCTION AND THE SEARCH FOR FOOD.

THESE MOVEMENTS ARE OFTEN GEOGRAPHICAL – FROM ONE REGION TO ANOTHER, MORE OR LESS DISTANT – BUT THEY CAN ALSO BE BATHYMETRIC, WITH VERTICAL MOVEMENT BETWEEN THE COAST AND DEEPER HABITATS.

WE'VE SEEN HOW NICOLE, A FEMALE GREAT WHITE, CROSSED THE INDIAN OCEAN.

BIRTH APRIL/AUGUST

TAGGING OTHER GREAT WHITES IN THE GUADALUPE ISLAND NATURE CONSERVANCY AREA HAS SHOWN THAT MALES MAKE ANNUAL ROUND TRIPS BETWEEN AN OCEANIC ZONE FAR OFF THE COAST, KNOWN AS "WHITE SHARK CAFÉ" AND THE ISLAND'S COASTAL ZONE, WHEREAS FEMALES, ONCE MATING IS OVER NEAR GUADALUPE, REMAIN OFFSHORE FOR THE ENTIRE GESTATIONAL PERIOD (FROM 16-18 MONTHS), RETURNING ONLY IN SPRING TO GIVE BIRTH IN THE GULF OF CALIFORNIA BEFORE RETURNING TO GUADALUPE FOR ANOTHER CYCLE.

MATING SEPT./OCTOBER

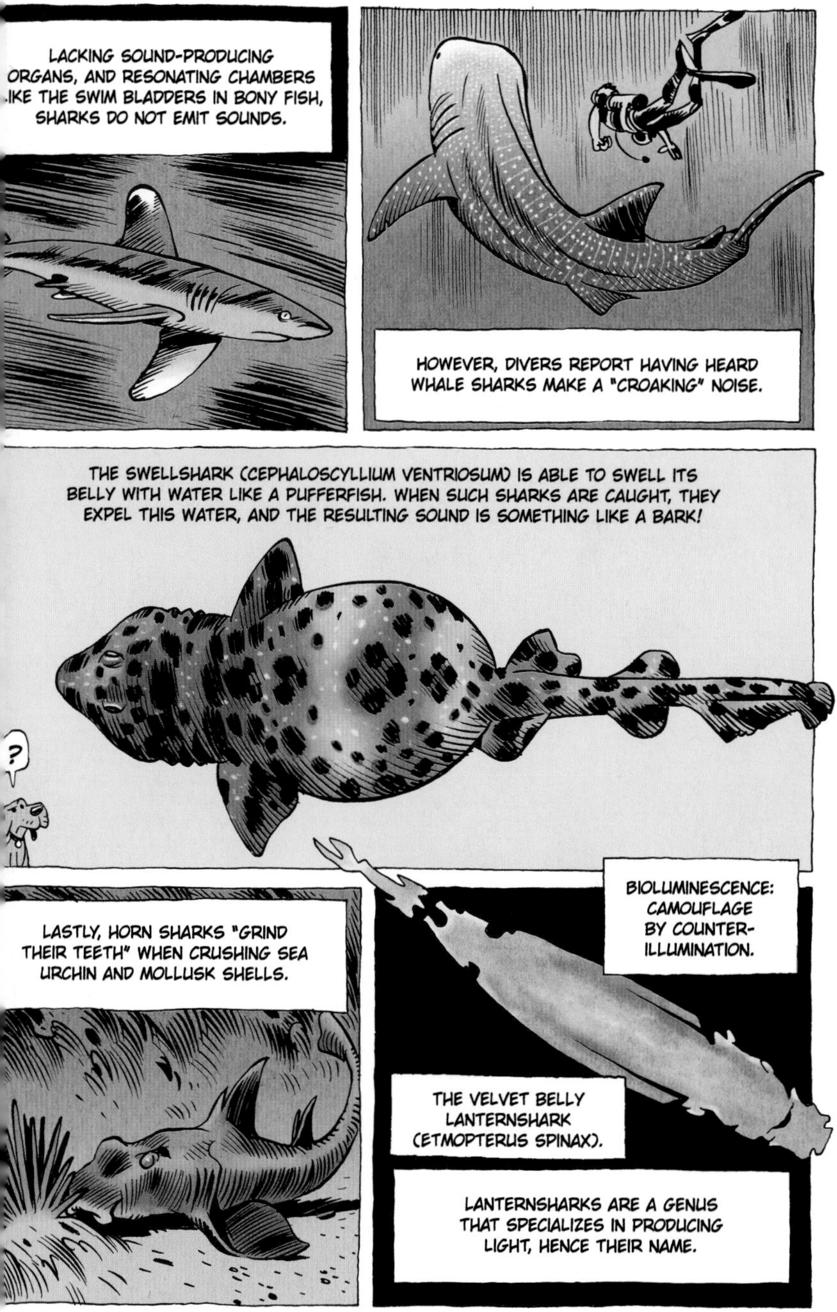
LACKING SOUND-PRODUCING ORGANS, AND RESONATING CHAMBERS IKE THE SWIM BLADDERS IN BONY FISH, SHARKS DO NOT EMIT SOUNDS.
HOWEVER, DIVERS REPORT HAVING HEARD WHALE SHARKS MAKE A "CROAKING" NOISE.
THE SWELLSHARK (CEPHALOSCYLLIUM VENTRIOSUM) IS ABLE TO SWELL ITS BELLY WITH WATER LIKE A PUFFERFISH. WHEN SUCH SHARKS ARE CAUGHT, THEY EXPEL THIS WATER, AND THE RESULTING SOUND IS SOMETHING LIKE A BARK!
?
LASTLY, HORN SHARKS "GRIND THEIR TEETH" WHEN CRUSHING SEA URCHIN AND MOLLUSK SHELLS.
BIOLUMINESCENCE: CAMOUFLAGE BY COUNTER-ILLUMINATION.
THE VELVET BELLY LANTERNSHARK (ETMOPTERUS SPINAX).
LANTERNSHARKS ARE A GENUS THAT SPECIALIZES IN PRODUCING LIGHT, HENCE THEIR NAME.

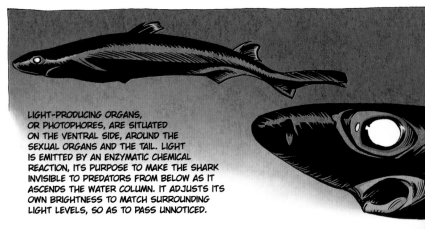

LIGHT-PRODUCING ORGANS, OR PHOTOPHORES, ARE SITUATED ON THE VENTRAL SIDE, AROUND THE SEXUAL ORGANS AND THE TAIL. LIGHT IS EMITTED BY AN ENZYMATIC CHEMICAL REACTION, ITS PURPOSE TO MAKE THE SHARK INVISIBLE TO PREDATORS FROM BELOW AS IT ASCENDS THE WATER COLUMN. IT ADJUSTS ITS OWN BRIGHTNESS TO MATCH SURROUNDING LIGHT LEVELS, SO AS TO PASS UNNOTICED.

ARE SHARKS "SOCIAL" CREATURES?

THEY HAVE A REPUTATION FOR BEING SOLITARY HUNTERS. HOWEVER, INSTANCES OF SOCIABILITY HAVE BEEN REPORTED.

SOME SHARK SPECIES ARE KNOWN TO FORM SCHOOLS OF UP TO SEVERAL HUNDRED INDIVIDUALS: FOR EXAMPLE, SCALLOPED HAMMERHEADS, SAND TIGER SHARKS, AND WHITETIP REEF SHARKS.

RECENTLY, IT WAS SHOWN THAT BLACKTIP REEF SHARKS (CARCHARHINUS MELANOPTERUS) FROM MO'OREA IN FRENCH POLYNESIA WERE ORGANIZED INTO "TRIBES," AND MOVEMENTS OBSERVED BETWEEN THESE GROUPS WERE NOT RANDOM, CORRESPONDING INSTEAD TO A HIERARCHY OF RELATIONSHIPS.

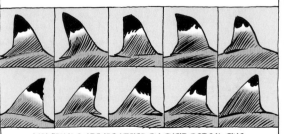

INDIVIDUALS ARE IDENTIFIED BY THEIR DORSAL FINS.

FIRST EVIDENCE THAT "SOCIAL NETWORKS" EXISTE[D] AMONG FISH!

HOW DO SHARKS COMMUNICATE?

THE MOST OBVIOUS FORM OF COMMUNICATION IS BODY LANGUAGE: THE BODY'S BEARING AND POSTURE ARE USED AS SIGNALS.

WHEN AN INTRUDER VENTURES INTO A GREY REEF SHARK'S (CARCHARHINUS AMBLYRHYNCHOS) TERRITORY, THEY BEGIN CIRCLING MENACINGLY, DROPPING THEIR PECTORAL FIN, AND "HUNCHING" THEIR BODIES.

COMMUNICATIONAL POSTURES HAVE RECENTLY BEEN OBSERVED AMONG THE GREAT WHITES OF SOUTH AFRICA: PARALLEL SWIMMING, SWIM-BYS, ETC. BUT WHETHER THIS CONSTITUTES A SPECIES-WIDE LANGUAGE HAS YET TO BE CONFIRMED.

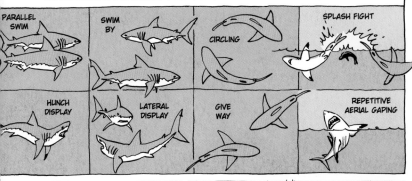

PARALLEL SWIM

SWIM BY

CIRCLING

SPLASH FIGHT

HUNCH DISPLAY

LATERAL DISPLAY

GIVE WAY

REPETITIVE AERIAL GAPING

AQUARIUM EXPERIMENTS ON SHARKS HAVE SUGGESTED ANOTHER FORM OF COMMUNICATION: THEY REACT TO CHEMICAL MESSAGES, OR PHEROMONES.

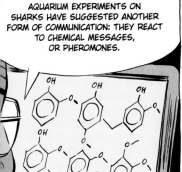

SO: ARE SHARKS "INTELLIGENT"?

OBVIOUSLY, WE CAN'T GIVE THEM IQ TESTS. BUT WE CAN GAUGE THEIR INTELLECTUAL CAPACITIES THROUGH MORE INDIRECT METHODS.

ONE ANATOMICAL METHODS CONSISTS OF CALCULATING THE RATIO BETWEEN BRAIN AND BODY WEIGHT, SINCE IT WOULD SEEM THAT HAVING A "BIG" BRAIN WOULD IMPLY INTELLIGENCE. IT'S SIMPLISTIC, BUT GIVES SOME IDEA, ALL THE SAME, OF INTELLECTUAL POTENTIAL.
BRAIN WEIGHT IN GRAMS
10,000
1,000
100
10
1
0,1
MAMMALS
ELASMOBRANCHS
BIRDS
FISH
0,001
0,01
0,1
1
10
100
1,000
10,000
BODY WEIGHT IN GRAMS
IN THIS GRAPH, WE CAN SEE THAT ELASMOBRANCHS (SHARKS AND RAYS) RATE RATHER WELL, AND HAVE RATIOS HIGHER THAN THOSE OF BONY FISH AND BIRDS—IN FACT, THE EQUAL OF MANY MAMMALS.
BUT WE MUST ALSO TAKE THE BRAIN'S STRUCTURE INTO ACCOUNT: A LARGE PART OF A SHARK'S BRAIN IS MADE UP OF OLFACTORY LOBES.
IF WE DEFINE ANIMAL INTELLIGENCE AS THE ABILITY TO ADAPT TO CHANGES IN THE ENVIRONMENT, THEN SHARKS COULD BE SEEN AS INTELLIGENT SINCE THEY'VE SURVIVED FIVE MAJOR EXTINCTION EVENTS!
WILL THEY MANAGE TO SURVIV A SIXTH, BROUGHT ABOUT BY HUMAN ACTIVITY?
OTHER OBSERVATIONS ATTEST FAVORABLY TO A CERTAIN INTELLIGENCE AMONG SHARKS.
THEY ARE CAPABLE OF LEARNING, ALTERING THEIR BEHAVIOR, AND MEMORIZING ACTIONS THAT ARE NOT HABITUAL FOR THEM. IN EXPERIMENTAL CONDITIONS, TESTS HAVE SHOWN THAT THEY CAN REMEMBER DRILLS AFTER A HIATUS OF SEVERAL MONTHS IN TRAINING.

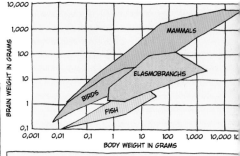

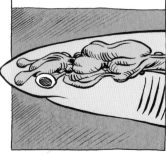

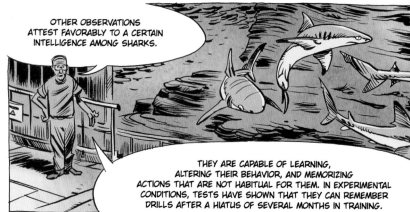

IN THEIR NATURAL SETTING, THEY SOON LEARN TO LOCATE "EASY" SOURCES OF FOOD, RETURNING REGULARLY TO IT.

WHEN DEVIL'S ISLAND WAS STILL A PRISON, THE BELL ANNOUNCING THE BURIAL AT SEA OF A DECEASED PRISONER WAS, FOR SHARKS, LIKE A HORN SOUNDING THE HUNT HAD BEGUN.

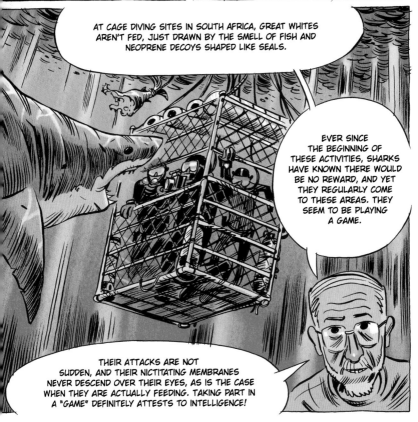

AT CAGE DIVING SITES IN SOUTH AFRICA, GREAT WHITES AREN'T FED, JUST DRAWN BY THE SMELL OF FISH AND NEOPRENE DECOYS SHAPED LIKE SEALS.

EVER SINCE THE BEGINNING OF THESE ACTIVITIES, SHARKS HAVE KNOWN THERE WOULD BE NO REWARD, AND YET THEY REGULARLY COME TO THESE AREAS. THEY SEEM TO BE PLAYING A GAME.

THEIR ATTACKS ARE NOT SUDDEN, AND THEIR NICTITATING MEMBRANES NEVER DESCEND OVER THEIR EYES, AS IS THE CASE WHEN THEY ARE ACTUALLY FEEDING. TAKING PART IN A "GAME" DEFINITELY ATTESTS TO INTELLIGENCE!

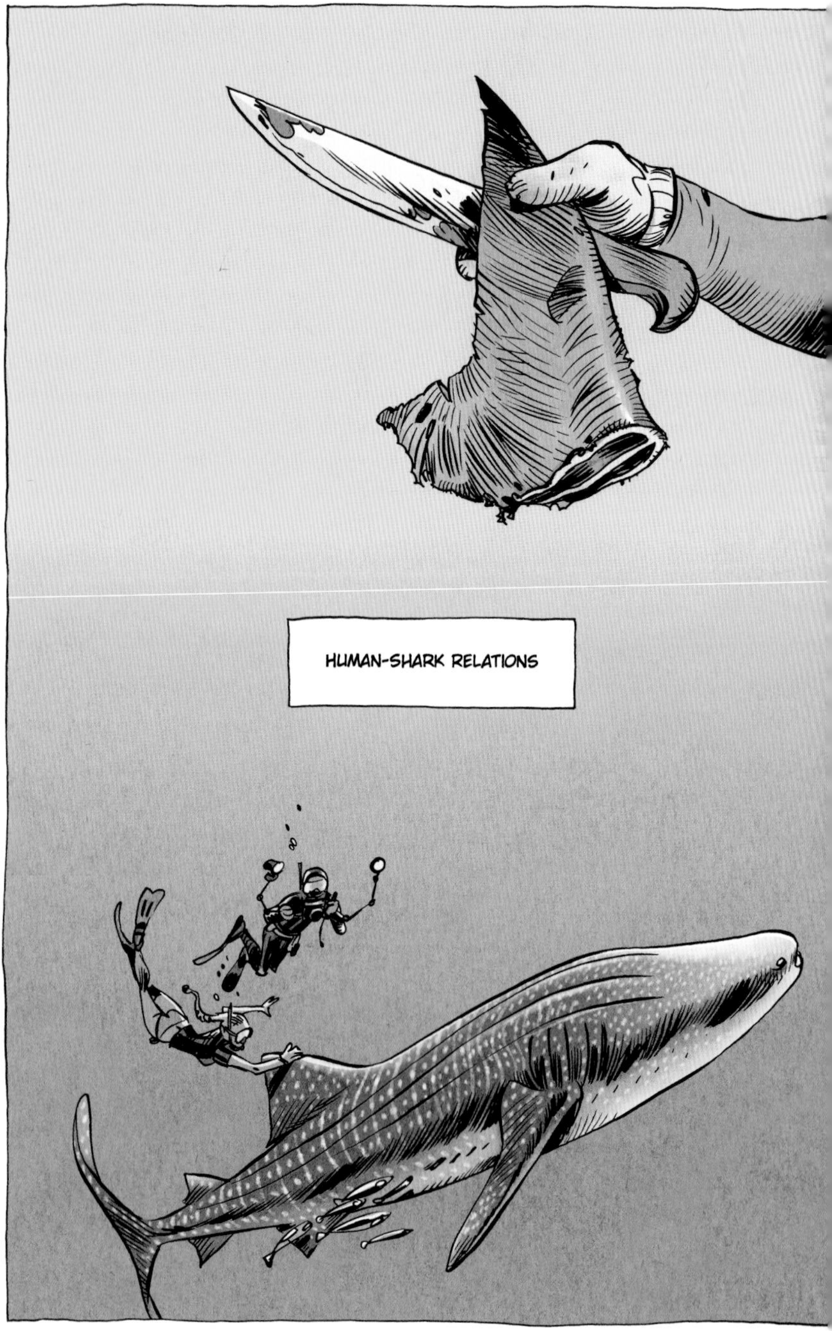
HUMAN-SHARK RELATIONS

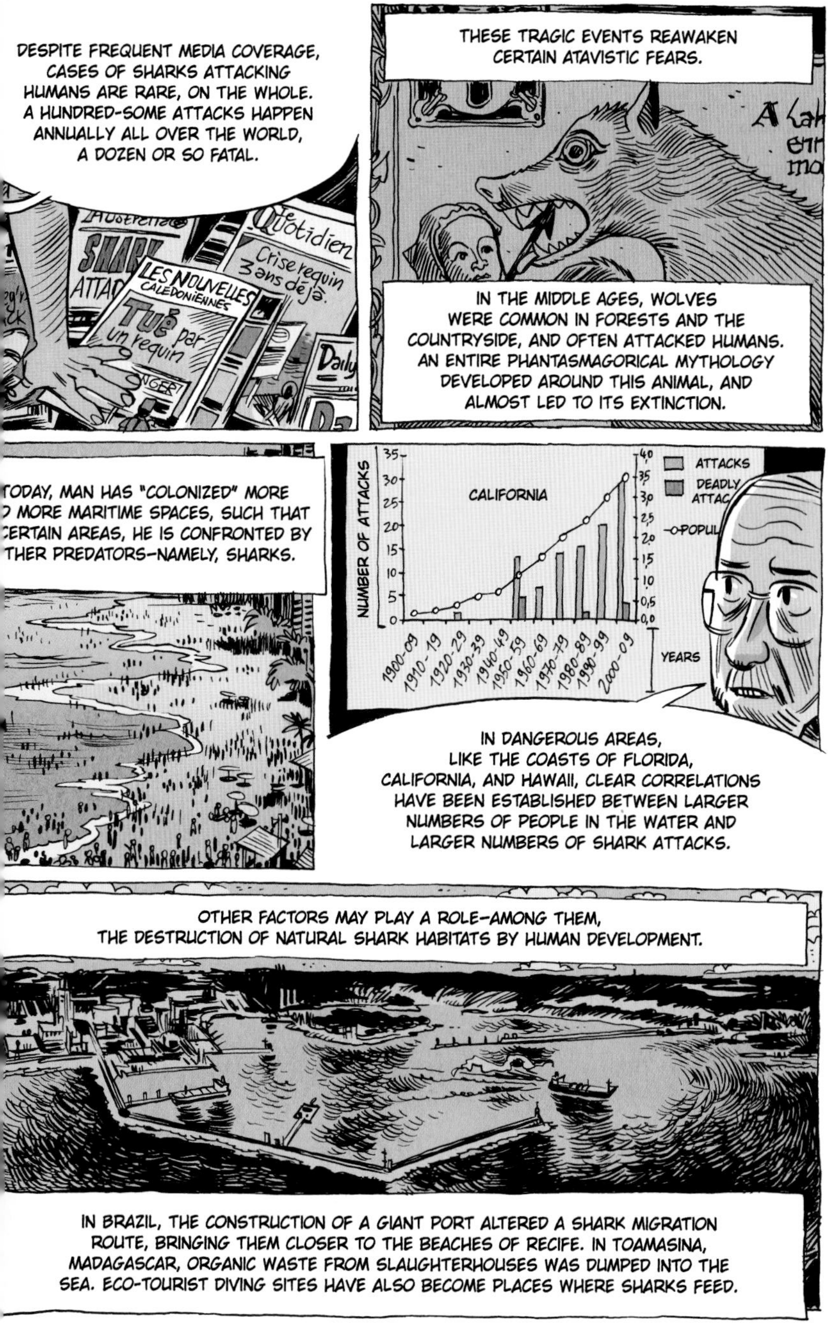
DESPITE FREQUENT MEDIA COVERAGE, CASES OF SHARKS ATTACKING HUMANS ARE RARE, ON THE WHOLE. A HUNDRED-SOME ATTACKS HAPPEN ANNUALLY ALL OVER THE WORLD, A DOZEN OR SO FATAL.
SHARK ATTAC
Le Quotidien
Crise requin 3 ans déjà
LES NOUVELLES CALEDONIENNES
Tué par un requin
Daily
THESE TRAGIC EVENTS REAWAKEN CERTAIN ATAVISTIC FEARS.
IN THE MIDDLE AGES, WOLVES WERE COMMON IN FORESTS AND THE COUNTRYSIDE, AND OFTEN ATTACKED HUMANS. AN ENTIRE PHANTASMAGORICAL MYTHOLOGY DEVELOPED AROUND THIS ANIMAL, AND ALMOST LED TO ITS EXTINCTION.
TODAY, MAN HAS "COLONIZED" MORE
MORE MARITIME SPACES, SUCH THAT
CERTAIN AREAS, HE IS CONFRONTED BY
THER PREDATORS—NAMELY, SHARKS.
CALIFORNIA
NUMBER OF ATTACKS
0 5 10 15 20 25 30 35
0,0 0,5 1,0 1,5 2,0 2,5 3,0 3,5 4,0
ATTACKS
DEADLY ATTAC
POPUL
1900-09 1910-19 1920-29 1930-39 1940-49 1950-59 1960-69 1970-79 1980-89 1990-99 2000-09
YEARS
IN DANGEROUS AREAS, LIKE THE COASTS OF FLORIDA, CALIFORNIA, AND HAWAII, CLEAR CORRELATIONS HAVE BEEN ESTABLISHED BETWEEN LARGER NUMBERS OF PEOPLE IN THE WATER AND LARGER NUMBERS OF SHARK ATTACKS.
OTHER FACTORS MAY PLAY A ROLE—AMONG THEM, THE DESTRUCTION OF NATURAL SHARK HABITATS BY HUMAN DEVELOPMENT.
IN BRAZIL, THE CONSTRUCTION OF A GIANT PORT ALTERED A SHARK MIGRATION ROUTE, BRINGING THEM CLOSER TO THE BEACHES OF RECIFE. IN TOAMASINA, MADAGASCAR, ORGANIC WASTE FROM SLAUGHTERHOUSES WAS DUMPED INTO THE SEA. ECO-TOURIST DIVING SITES HAVE ALSO BECOME PLACES WHERE SHARKS FEED.

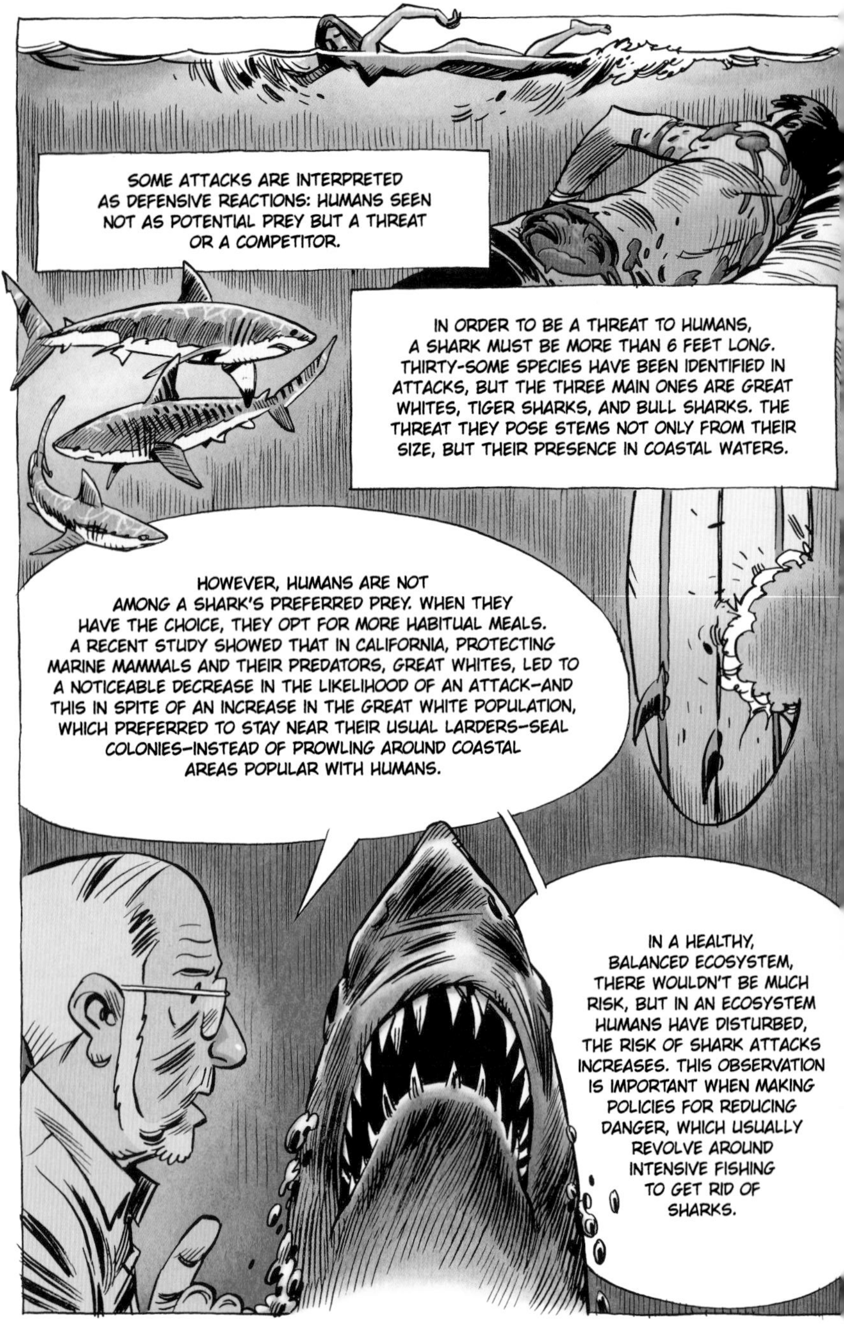
SOME ATTACKS ARE INTERPRETED AS DEFENSIVE REACTIONS: HUMANS SEEN NOT AS POTENTIAL PREY BUT A THREAT OR A COMPETITOR.
IN ORDER TO BE A THREAT TO HUMANS, A SHARK MUST BE MORE THAN 6 FEET LONG. THIRTY-SOME SPECIES HAVE BEEN IDENTIFIED IN ATTACKS, BUT THE THREE MAIN ONES ARE GREAT WHITES, TIGER SHARKS, AND BULL SHARKS. THE THREAT THEY POSE STEMS NOT ONLY FROM THEIR SIZE, BUT THEIR PRESENCE IN COASTAL WATERS.
HOWEVER, HUMANS ARE NOT AMONG A SHARK'S PREFERRED PREY. WHEN THEY HAVE THE CHOICE, THEY OPT FOR MORE HABITUAL MEALS. A RECENT STUDY SHOWED THAT IN CALIFORNIA, PROTECTING MARINE MAMMALS AND THEIR PREDATORS, GREAT WHITES, LED TO A NOTICEABLE DECREASE IN THE LIKELIHOOD OF AN ATTACK—AND THIS IN SPITE OF AN INCREASE IN THE GREAT WHITE POPULATION, WHICH PREFERRED TO STAY NEAR THEIR USUAL LARDERS—SEAL COLONIES—INSTEAD OF PROWLING AROUND COASTAL AREAS POPULAR WITH HUMANS.
IN A HEALTHY, BALANCED ECOSYSTEM, THERE WOULDN'T BE MUCH RISK, BUT IN AN ECOSYSTEM HUMANS HAVE DISTURBED, THE RISK OF SHARK ATTACKS INCREASES. THIS OBSERVATION IS IMPORTANT WHEN MAKING POLICIES FOR REDUCING DANGER, WHICH USUALLY REVOLVE AROUND INTENSIVE FISHING TO GET RID OF SHARKS.

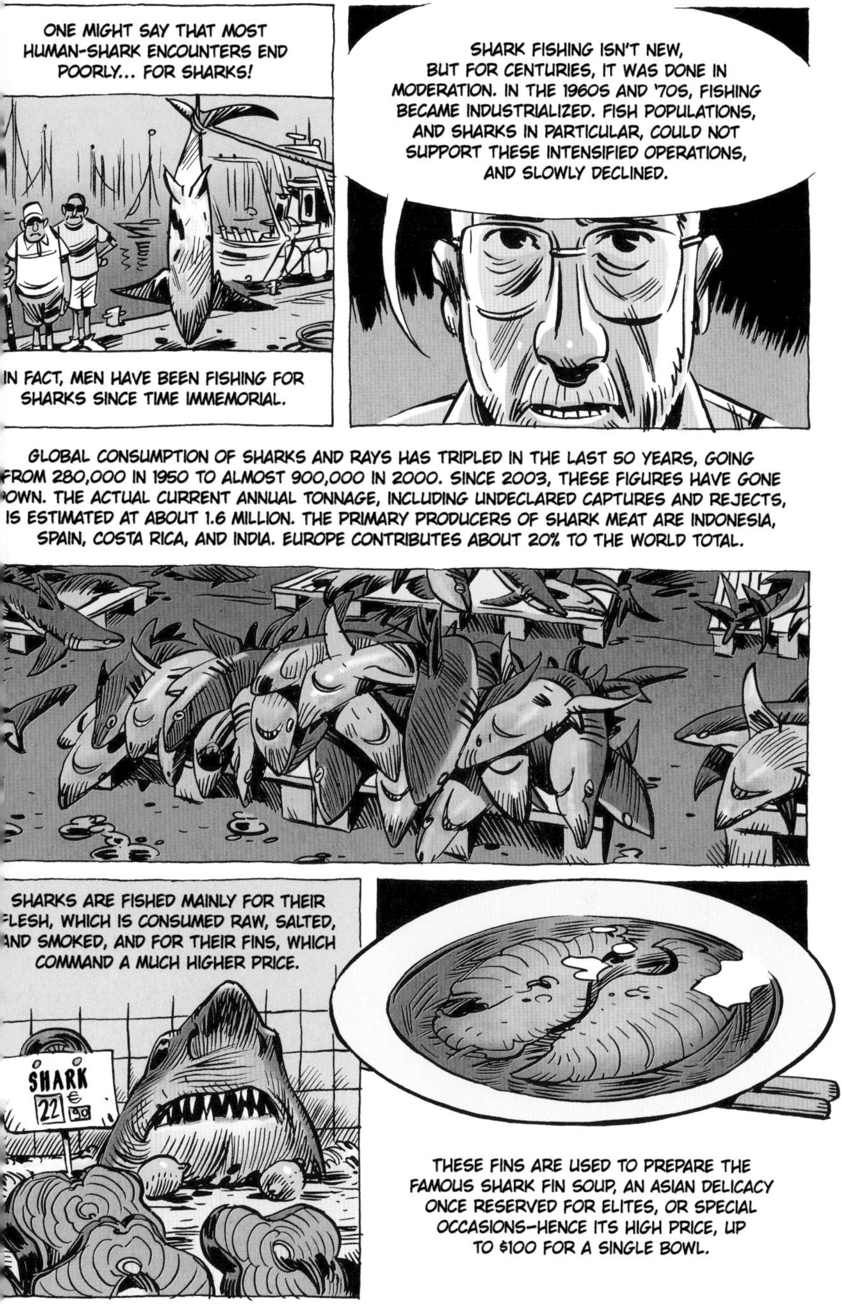
ONE MIGHT SAY THAT MOST HUMAN-SHARK ENCOUNTERS END POORLY... FOR SHARKS!
IN FACT, MEN HAVE BEEN FISHING FOR SHARKS SINCE TIME IMMEMORIAL.
SHARK FISHING ISN'T NEW, BUT FOR CENTURIES, IT WAS DONE IN MODERATION. IN THE 1960S AND '70S, FISHING BECAME INDUSTRIALIZED. FISH POPULATIONS, AND SHARKS IN PARTICULAR, COULD NOT SUPPORT THESE INTENSIFIED OPERATIONS, AND SLOWLY DECLINED.
GLOBAL CONSUMPTION OF SHARKS AND RAYS HAS TRIPLED IN THE LAST 50 YEARS, GOING FROM 280,000 IN 1950 TO ALMOST 900,000 IN 2000. SINCE 2003, THESE FIGURES HAVE GONE OWN. THE ACTUAL CURRENT ANNUAL TONNAGE, INCLUDING UNDECLARED CAPTURES AND REJECTS, IS ESTIMATED AT ABOUT 1.6 MILLION. THE PRIMARY PRODUCERS OF SHARK MEAT ARE INDONESIA, SPAIN, COSTA RICA, AND INDIA. EUROPE CONTRIBUTES ABOUT 20% TO THE WORLD TOTAL.
SHARKS ARE FISHED MAINLY FOR THEIR FLESH, WHICH IS CONSUMED RAW, SALTED, ND SMOKED, AND FOR THEIR FINS, WHICH COMMAND A MUCH HIGHER PRICE.
SHARK
22 € 90
THESE FINS ARE USED TO PREPARE THE FAMOUS SHARK FIN SOUP, AN ASIAN DELICACY ONCE RESERVED FOR ELITES, OR SPECIAL OCCASIONS—HENCE ITS HIGH PRICE, UP TO $100 FOR A SINGLE BOWL.

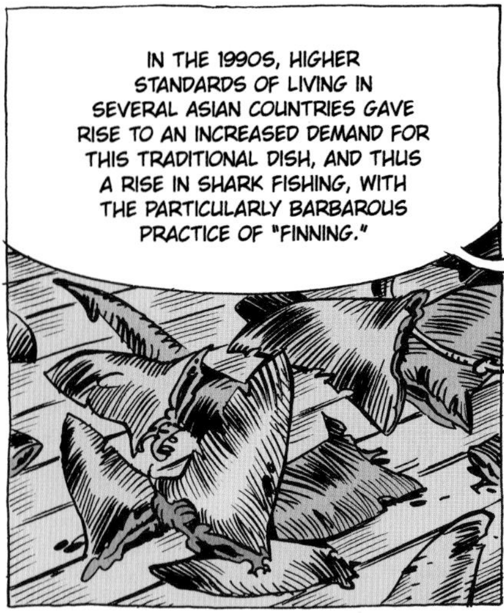
IN THE 1990S, HIGHER STANDARDS OF LIVING IN SEVERAL ASIAN COUNTRIES GAVE RISE TO AN INCREASED DEMAND FOR THIS TRADITIONAL DISH, AND THUS A RISE IN SHARK FISHING, WITH THE PARTICULARLY BARBAROUS PRACTICE OF "FINNING."

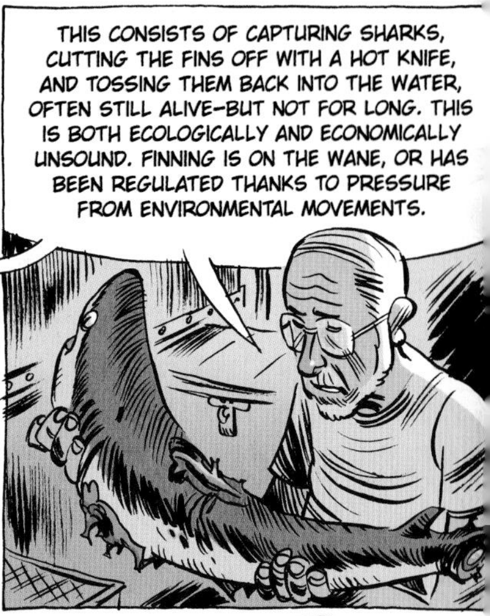
THIS CONSISTS OF CAPTURING SHARKS, CUTTING THE FINS OFF WITH A HOT KNIFE, AND TOSSING THEM BACK INTO THE WATER, OFTEN STILL ALIVE—BUT NOT FOR LONG. THIS IS BOTH ECOLOGICALLY AND ECONOMICALLY UNSOUND. FINNING IS ON THE WANE, OR HAS BEEN REGULATED THANKS TO PRESSURE FROM ENVIRONMENTAL MOVEMENTS.

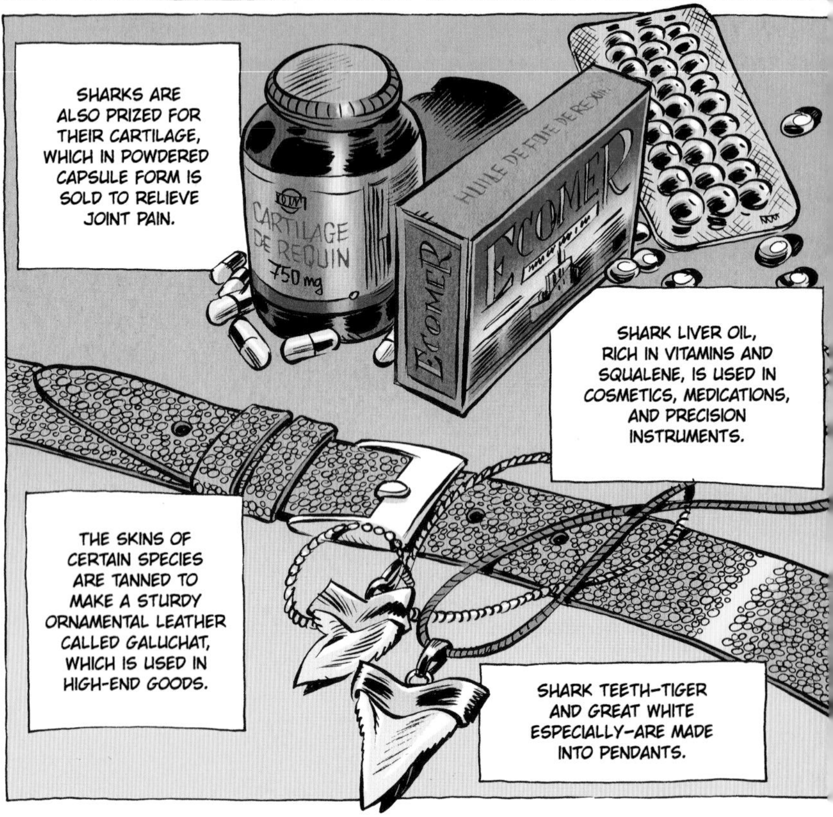
SHARKS ARE ALSO PRIZED FOR THEIR CARTILAGE, WHICH IN POWDERED CAPSULE FORM IS SOLD TO RELIEVE JOINT PAIN.
CARTILAGE DE REQUIN
750 mg
HUILE DE FOIE DE REQUIN
ECOMER
SHARK LIVER OIL, RICH IN VITAMINS AND SQUALENE, IS USED IN COSMETICS, MEDICATIONS, AND PRECISION INSTRUMENTS.
THE SKINS OF CERTAIN SPECIES ARE TANNED TO MAKE A STURDY ORNAMENTAL LEATHER CALLED GALUCHAT, WHICH IS USED IN HIGH-END GOODS.
SHARK TEETH—TIGER AND GREAT WHITE ESPECIALLY—ARE MADE INTO PENDANTS.

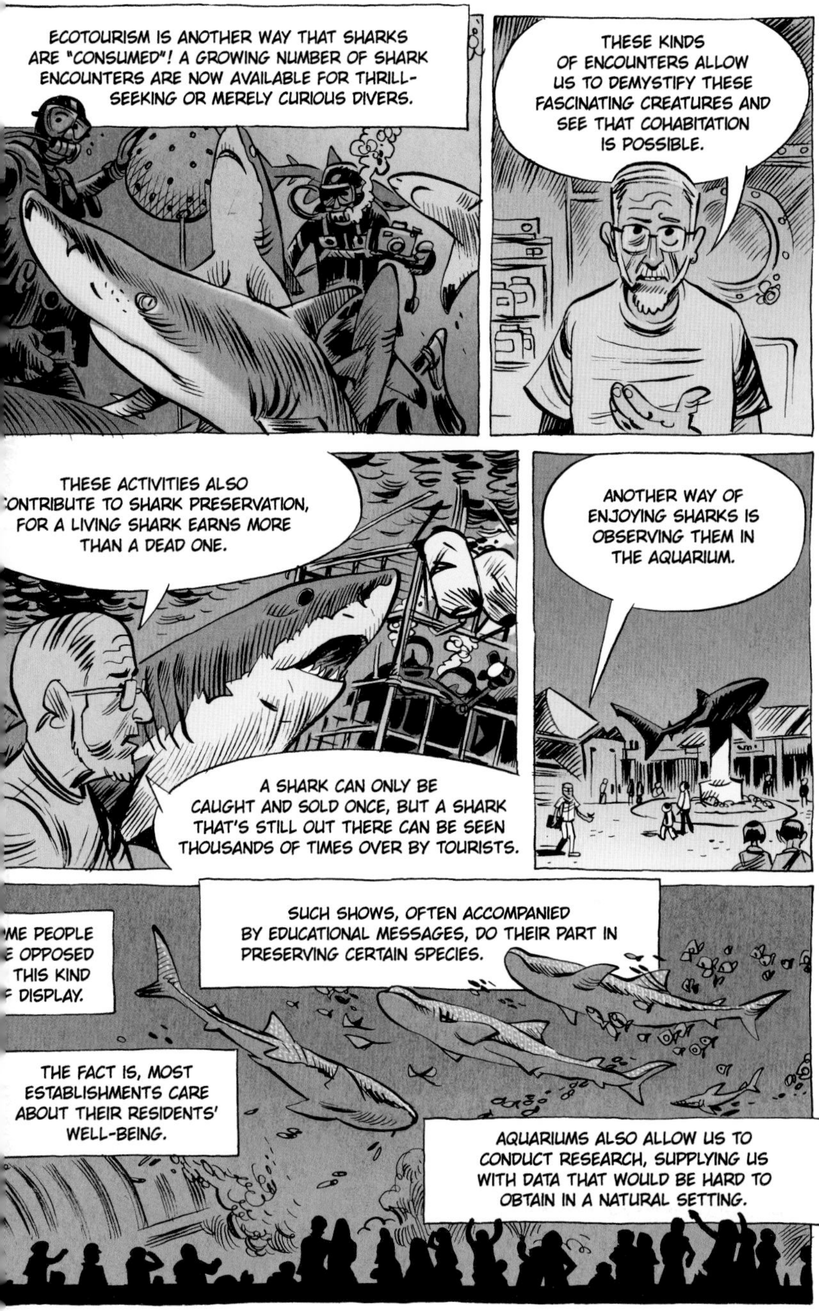
ECOTOURISM IS ANOTHER WAY THAT SHARKS ARE "CONSUMED"! A GROWING NUMBER OF SHARK ENCOUNTERS ARE NOW AVAILABLE FOR THRILL-SEEKING OR MERELY CURIOUS DIVERS.
THESE KINDS OF ENCOUNTERS ALLOW US TO DEMYSTIFY THESE FASCINATING CREATURES AND SEE THAT COHABITATION IS POSSIBLE.
THESE ACTIVITIES ALSO CONTRIBUTE TO SHARK PRESERVATION, FOR A LIVING SHARK EARNS MORE THAN A DEAD ONE.
A SHARK CAN ONLY BE CAUGHT AND SOLD ONCE, BUT A SHARK THAT'S STILL OUT THERE CAN BE SEEN THOUSANDS OF TIMES OVER BY TOURISTS.
ANOTHER WAY OF ENJOYING SHARKS IS OBSERVING THEM IN THE AQUARIUM.
ME PEOPLE E OPPOSED THIS KIND F DISPLAY.
SUCH SHOWS, OFTEN ACCOMPANIED BY EDUCATIONAL MESSAGES, DO THEIR PART IN PRESERVING CERTAIN SPECIES.
THE FACT IS, MOST ESTABLISHMENTS CARE ABOUT THEIR RESIDENTS' WELL-BEING.
AQUARIUMS ALSO ALLOW US TO CONDUCT RESEARCH, SUPPLYING US WITH DATA THAT WOULD BE HARD TO OBTAIN IN A NATURAL SETTING.

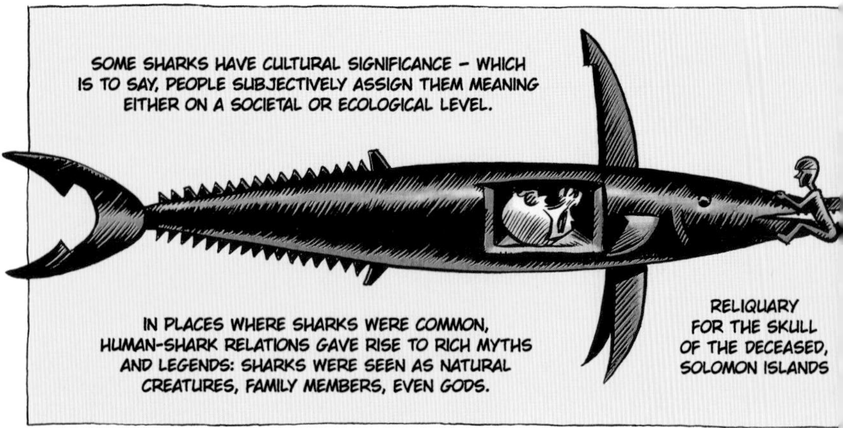
SOME SHARKS HAVE CULTURAL SIGNIFICANCE – WHICH IS TO SAY, PEOPLE SUBJECTIVELY ASSIGN THEM MEANING EITHER ON A SOCIETAL OR ECOLOGICAL LEVEL.
IN PLACES WHERE SHARKS WERE COMMON, HUMAN-SHARK RELATIONS GAVE RISE TO RICH MYTHS AND LEGENDS: SHARKS WERE SEEN AS NATURAL CREATURES, FAMILY MEMBERS, EVEN GODS.
RELIQUARY FOR THE SKULL OF THE DECEASED, SOLOMON ISLANDS

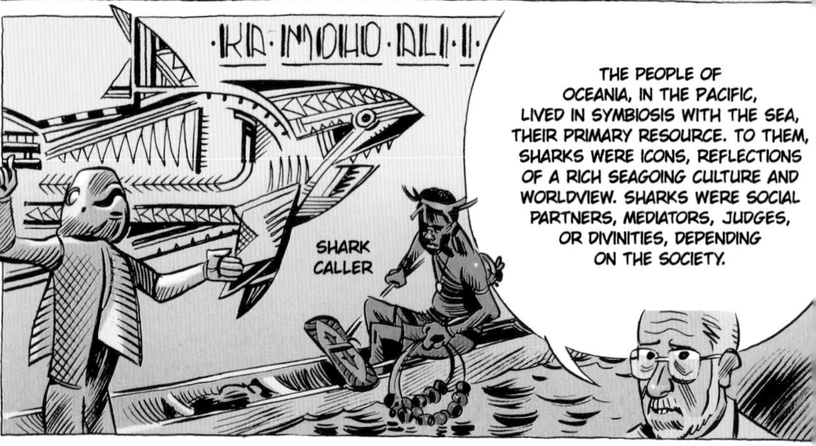
·KA·MOHO·ALI·I·
SHARK CALLER
THE PEOPLE OF OCEANIA, IN THE PACIFIC, LIVED IN SYMBIOSIS WITH THE SEA, THEIR PRIMARY RESOURCE. TO THEM, SHARKS WERE ICONS, REFLECTIONS OF A RICH SEAGOING CULTURE AND WORLDVIEW. SHARKS WERE SOCIAL PARTNERS, MEDIATORS, JUDGES, OR DIVINITIES, DEPENDING ON THE SOCIETY.

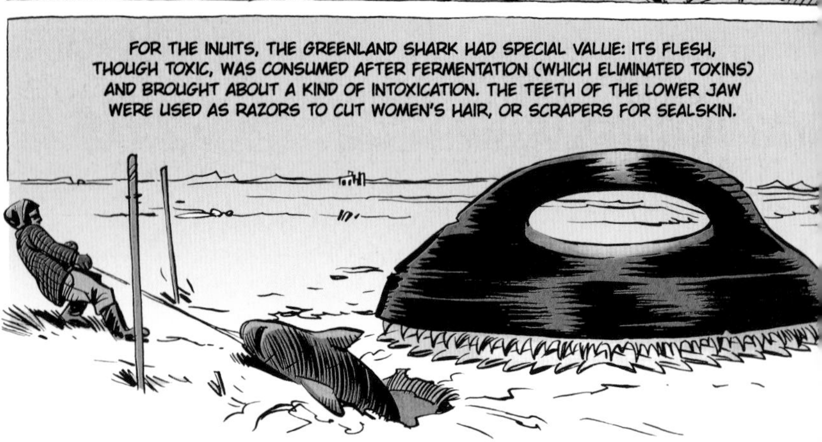
FOR THE INUITS, THE GREENLAND SHARK HAD SPECIAL VALUE: ITS FLESH, THOUGH TOXIC, WAS CONSUMED AFTER FERMENTATION (WHICH ELIMINATED TOXINS) AND BROUGHT ABOUT A KIND OF INTOXICATION. THE TEETH OF THE LOWER JAW WERE USED AS RAZORS TO CUT WOMEN'S HAIR, OR SCRAPERS FOR SEALSKIN.

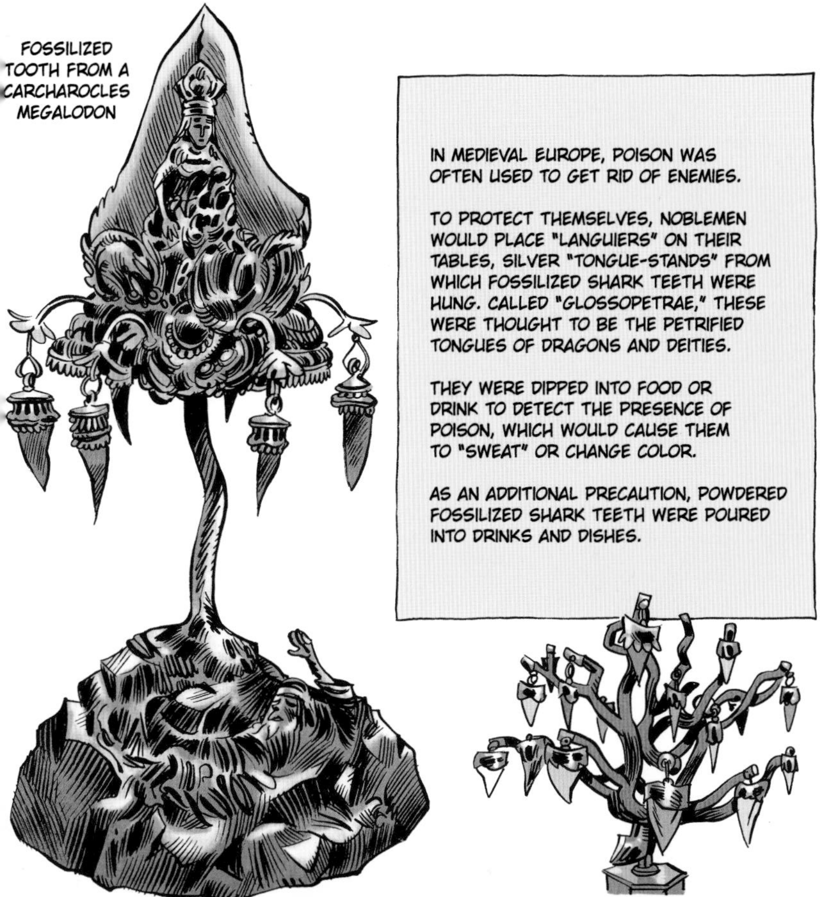
FOSSILIZED TOOTH FROM A CARCHAROCLES MEGALODON
IN MEDIEVAL EUROPE, POISON WAS OFTEN USED TO GET RID OF ENEMIES.
TO PROTECT THEMSELVES, NOBLEMEN WOULD PLACE "LANGUIERS" ON THEIR TABLES, SILVER "TONGUE-STANDS" FROM WHICH FOSSILIZED SHARK TEETH WERE HUNG. CALLED "GLOSSOPETRAE," THESE WERE THOUGHT TO BE THE PETRIFIED TONGUES OF DRAGONS AND DEITIES.
THEY WERE DIPPED INTO FOOD OR DRINK TO DETECT THE PRESENCE OF POISON, WHICH WOULD CAUSE THEM TO "SWEAT" OR CHANGE COLOR.
AS AN ADDITIONAL PRECAUTION, POWDERED FOSSILIZED SHARK TEETH WERE POURED INTO DRINKS AND DISHES.

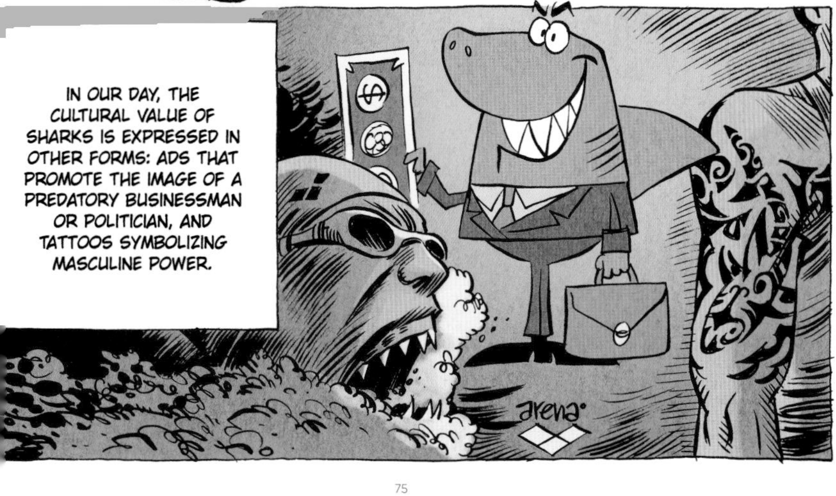
IN OUR DAY, THE CULTURAL VALUE OF SHARKS IS EXPRESSED IN OTHER FORMS: ADS THAT PROMOTE THE IMAGE OF A PREDATORY BUSINESSMAN OR POLITICIAN, AND TATTOOS SYMBOLIZING MASCULINE POWER.
arena

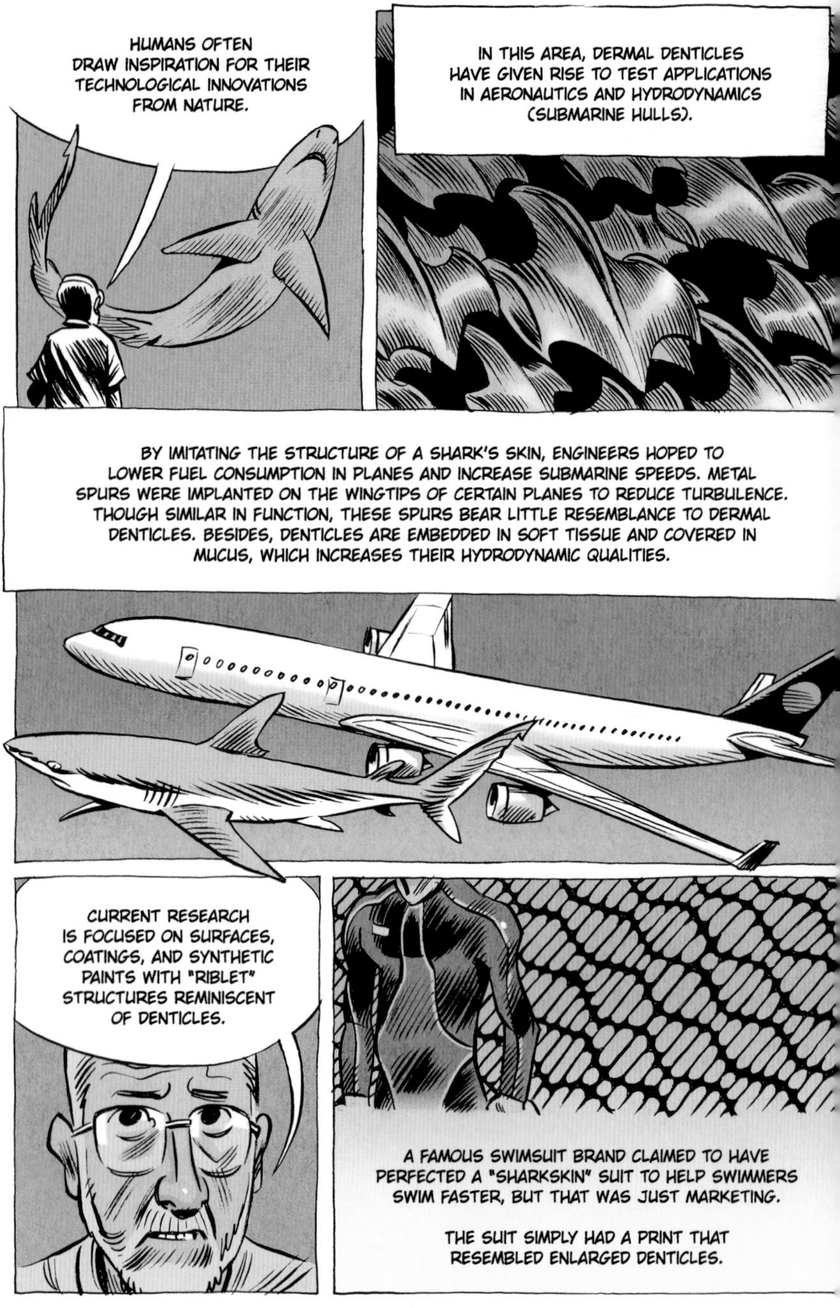

HUMANS OFTEN DRAW INSPIRATION FOR THEIR TECHNOLOGICAL INNOVATIONS FROM NATURE.
IN THIS AREA, DERMAL DENTICLES HAVE GIVEN RISE TO TEST APPLICATIONS IN AERONAUTICS AND HYDRODYNAMICS (SUBMARINE HULLS).
BY IMITATING THE STRUCTURE OF A SHARK'S SKIN, ENGINEERS HOPED TO LOWER FUEL CONSUMPTION IN PLANES AND INCREASE SUBMARINE SPEEDS. METAL SPURS WERE IMPLANTED ON THE WINGTIPS OF CERTAIN PLANES TO REDUCE TURBULENCE. THOUGH SIMILAR IN FUNCTION, THESE SPURS BEAR LITTLE RESEMBLANCE TO DERMAL DENTICLES. BESIDES, DENTICLES ARE EMBEDDED IN SOFT TISSUE AND COVERED IN MUCUS, WHICH INCREASES THEIR HYDRODYNAMIC QUALITIES.
CURRENT RESEARCH IS FOCUSED ON SURFACES, COATINGS, AND SYNTHETIC PAINTS WITH "RIBLET" STRUCTURES REMINISCENT OF DENTICLES.
A FAMOUS SWIMSUIT BRAND CLAIMED TO HAVE PERFECTED A "SHARKSKIN" SUIT TO HELP SWIMMERS SWIM FASTER, BUT THAT WAS JUST MARKETING.
THE SUIT SIMPLY HAD A PRINT THAT RESEMBLED ENLARGED DENTICLES.

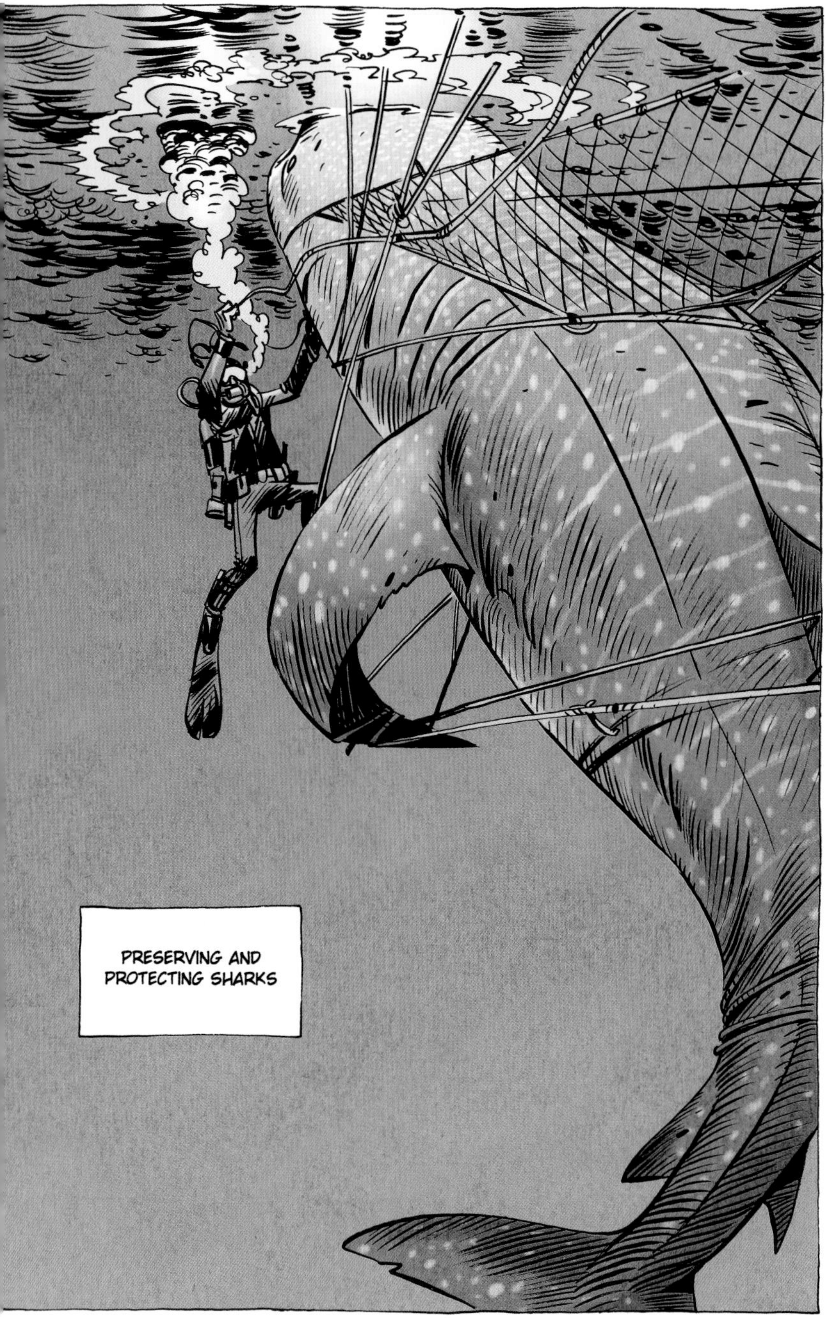
PRESERVING AND
PROTECTING SHARKS

ONE REASON FOR THE RECENT INTEREST IN SHARKS IS THE HIGHLIGHTING OF THEIR ECOLOGICAL ROLE IN MARINE FOOD CHAINS.

AMERICAN RESEARCHERS HAVE SHOWN THAT THE COLLAPSE OF A LONG-ESTABLISHED SCALLOP FISHERY WAS DUE TO OVERFISHING OF COASTAL SHARKS, WHICH FED ON RAYS, WHICH FED IN TURN ON SCALLOPS.

A DECLINE IN THE SHARK POPULATION ALLOWED RAY POPULATIONS TO SKYROCKET, LEADING TO A GREATER CONSUMPTION OF SCALLOPS, WHICH BECAME INSUFFICIENT FOR THE FISHERY TO REMAIN VIABLE.

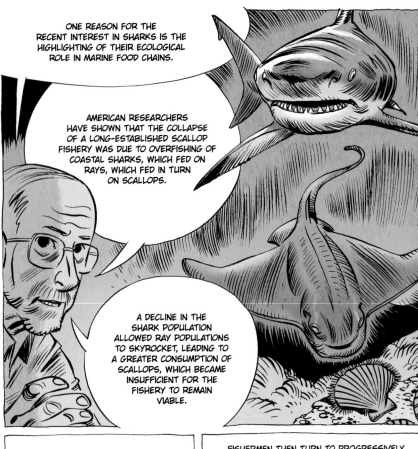

FISHING BEGINS WITH LARGER FISH (TUNA, GROUPER, SHARKS, ETC.) BECAUSE THEY ARE EASIER TO CATCH, AND HAVE HIGHER MARKET VALUE.

FISHERMEN THEN TURN TO PROGRESSIVELY LOWER RUNGS. LITTLE BY LITTLE, THE ECOSYSTEM BECOMES IMPOVERISHED, AND IN THE END, CONSISTS ENTIRELY OF SMALL FRY, PLANKTON, AND NOTABLE PROLIFERATIONS OF JELLYFISH AND DEEP-SEA INVERTEBRATES!

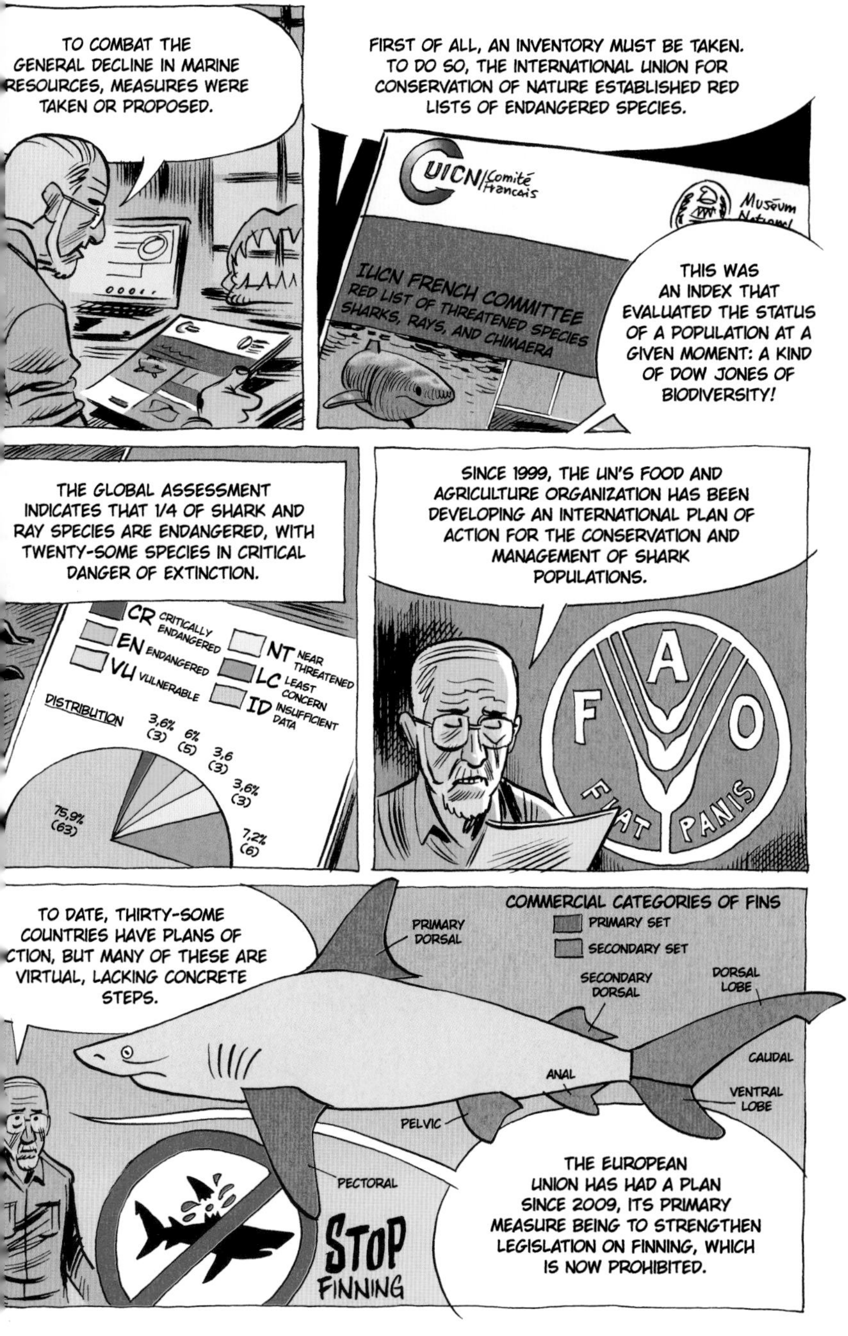
TO COMBAT THE GENERAL DECLINE IN MARINE RESOURCES, MEASURES WERE TAKEN OR PROPOSED.
FIRST OF ALL, AN INVENTORY MUST BE TAKEN. TO DO SO, THE INTERNATIONAL UNION FOR CONSERVATION OF NATURE ESTABLISHED RED LISTS OF ENDANGERED SPECIES.
UICN Comité Français
Muséum
IUCN FRENCH COMMITTEE
RED LIST OF THREATENED SPECIES
SHARKS, RAYS, AND CHIMAERA
THIS WAS AN INDEX THAT EVALUATED THE STATUS OF A POPULATION AT A GIVEN MOMENT: A KIND OF DOW JONES OF BIODIVERSITY!
THE GLOBAL ASSESSMENT INDICATES THAT 1/4 OF SHARK AND RAY SPECIES ARE ENDANGERED, WITH TWENTY-SOME SPECIES IN CRITICAL DANGER OF EXTINCTION.
CR CRITICALLY ENDANGERED
EN ENDANGERED
VU VULNERABLE
NT NEAR THREATENED
LC LEAST CONCERN
ID INSUFFICIENT DATA
DISTRIBUTION
3,6% (3)
6% (5)
3,6 (3)
3,6% (3)
7,2% (6)
75,9% (63)
SINCE 1999, THE UN'S FOOD AND AGRICULTURE ORGANIZATION HAS BEEN DEVELOPING AN INTERNATIONAL PLAN OF ACTION FOR THE CONSERVATION AND MANAGEMENT OF SHARK POPULATIONS.
F A O
FIAT PANIS
TO DATE, THIRTY-SOME COUNTRIES HAVE PLANS OF ACTION, BUT MANY OF THESE ARE VIRTUAL, LACKING CONCRETE STEPS.
COMMERCIAL CATEGORIES OF FINS
PRIMARY SET
SECONDARY SET
PRIMARY DORSAL
SECONDARY DORSAL
DORSAL LOBE
CAUDAL
ANAL
VENTRAL LOBE
PELVIC
PECTORAL
STOP FINNING
THE EUROPEAN UNION HAS HAD A PLAN SINCE 2009, ITS PRIMARY MEASURE BEING TO STRENGTHEN LEGISLATION ON FINNING, WHICH IS NOW PROHIBITED.

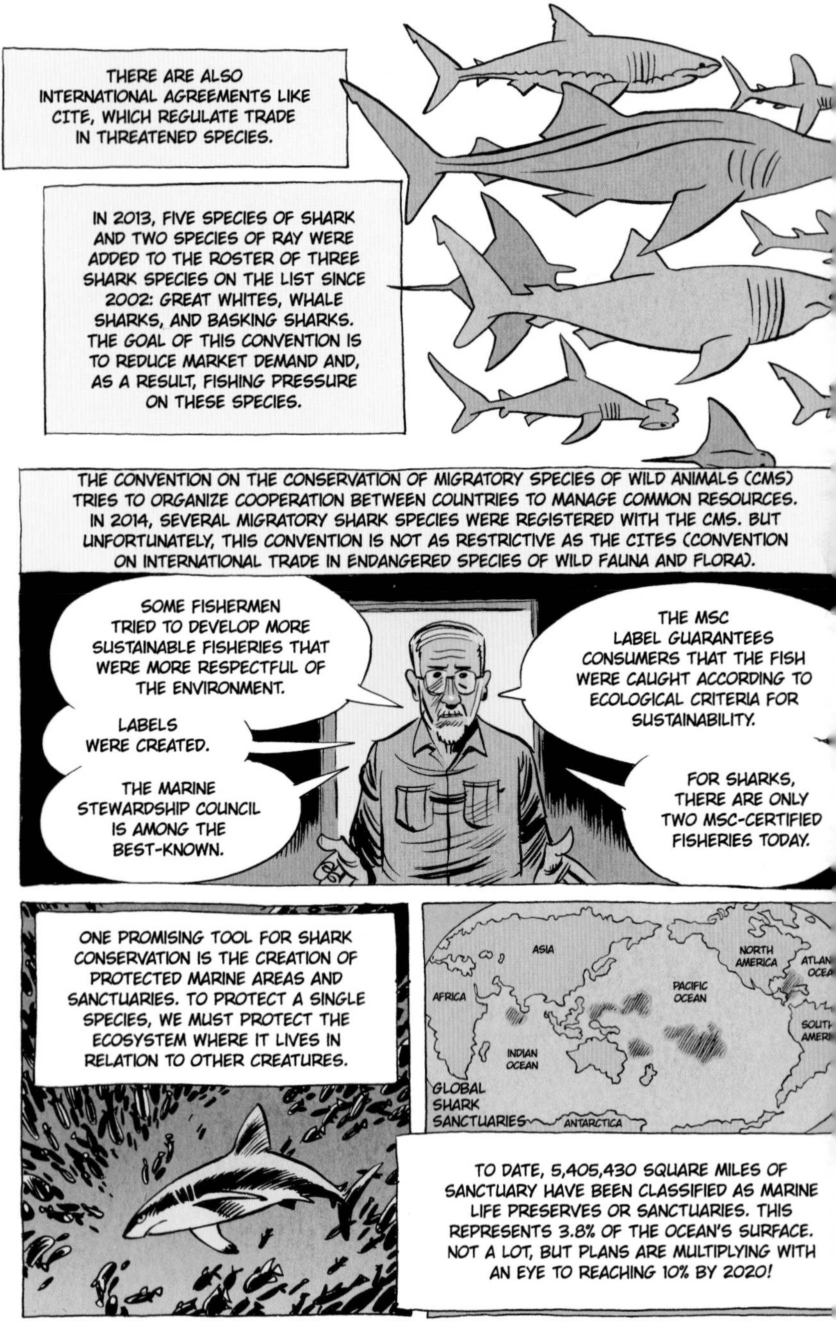
THERE ARE ALSO INTERNATIONAL AGREEMENTS LIKE CITE, WHICH REGULATE TRADE IN THREATENED SPECIES.
IN 2013, FIVE SPECIES OF SHARK AND TWO SPECIES OF RAY WERE ADDED TO THE ROSTER OF THREE SHARK SPECIES ON THE LIST SINCE 2002: GREAT WHITES, WHALE SHARKS, AND BASKING SHARKS. THE GOAL OF THIS CONVENTION IS TO REDUCE MARKET DEMAND AND, AS A RESULT, FISHING PRESSURE ON THESE SPECIES.
THE CONVENTION ON THE CONSERVATION OF MIGRATORY SPECIES OF WILD ANIMALS (CMS) TRIES TO ORGANIZE COOPERATION BETWEEN COUNTRIES TO MANAGE COMMON RESOURCES. IN 2014, SEVERAL MIGRATORY SHARK SPECIES WERE REGISTERED WITH THE CMS. BUT UNFORTUNATELY, THIS CONVENTION IS NOT AS RESTRICTIVE AS THE CITES (CONVENTION ON INTERNATIONAL TRADE IN ENDANGERED SPECIES OF WILD FAUNA AND FLORA).
SOME FISHERMEN TRIED TO DEVELOP MORE SUSTAINABLE FISHERIES THAT WERE MORE RESPECTFUL OF THE ENVIRONMENT.
LABELS WERE CREATED.
THE MARINE STEWARDSHIP COUNCIL IS AMONG THE BEST-KNOWN.
THE MSC LABEL GUARANTEES CONSUMERS THAT THE FISH WERE CAUGHT ACCORDING TO ECOLOGICAL CRITERIA FOR SUSTAINABILITY.
FOR SHARKS, THERE ARE ONLY TWO MSC-CERTIFIED FISHERIES TODAY.
ONE PROMISING TOOL FOR SHARK CONSERVATION IS THE CREATION OF PROTECTED MARINE AREAS AND SANCTUARIES. TO PROTECT A SINGLE SPECIES, WE MUST PROTECT THE ECOSYSTEM WHERE IT LIVES IN RELATION TO OTHER CREATURES.
ASIA
NORTH AMERICA
AFRICA
PACIFIC OCEAN
INDIAN OCEAN
GLOBAL SHARK SANCTUARIES
ANTARCTICA
TO DATE, 5,405,430 SQUARE MILES OF SANCTUARY HAVE BEEN CLASSIFIED AS MARINE LIFE PRESERVES OR SANCTUARIES. THIS REPRESENTS 3.8% OF THE OCEAN'S SURFACE. NOT A LOT, BUT PLANS ARE MULTIPLYING WITH AN EYE TO REACHING 10% BY 2020!

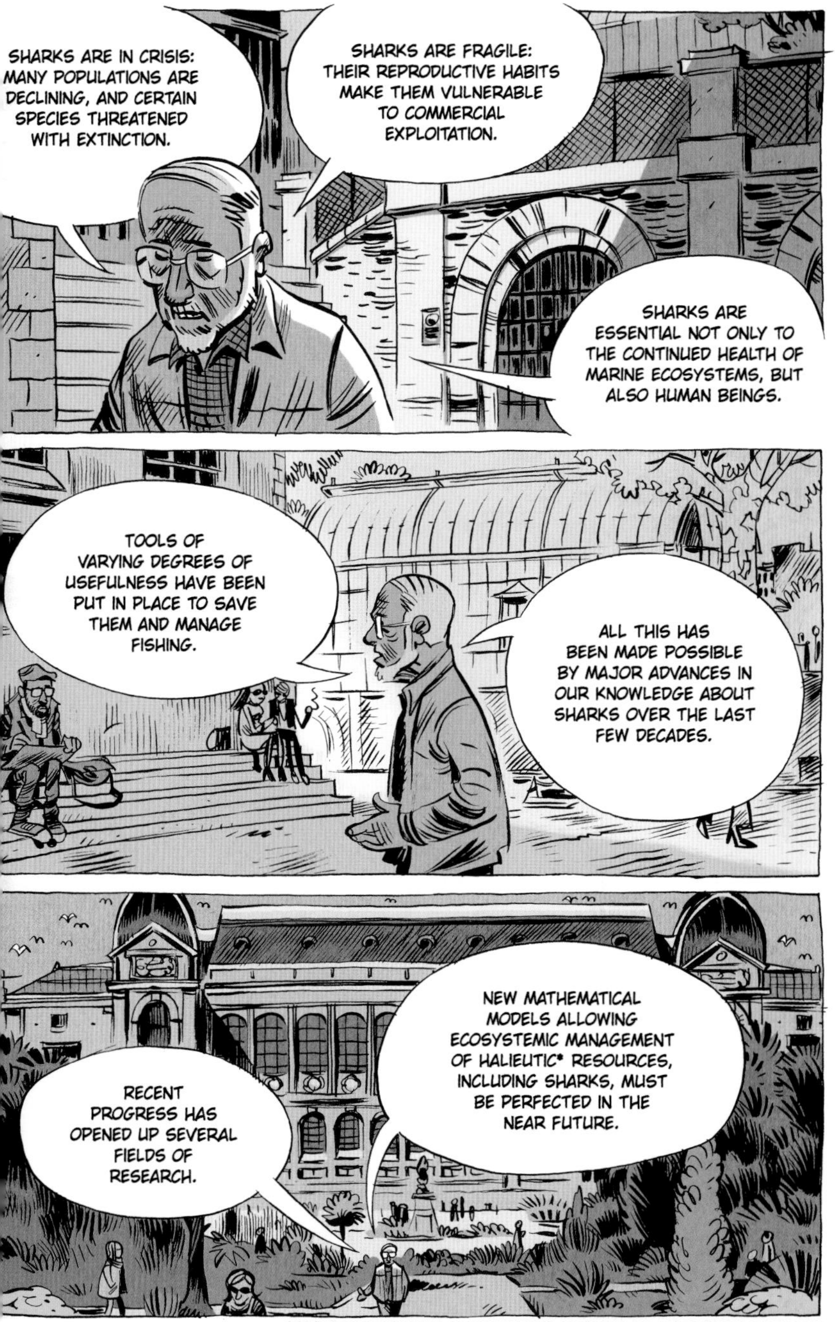
SHARKS ARE IN CRISIS: MANY POPULATIONS ARE DECLINING, AND CERTAIN SPECIES THREATENED WITH EXTINCTION.
SHARKS ARE FRAGILE: THEIR REPRODUCTIVE HABITS MAKE THEM VULNERABLE TO COMMERCIAL EXPLOITATION.
SHARKS ARE ESSENTIAL NOT ONLY TO THE CONTINUED HEALTH OF MARINE ECOSYSTEMS, BUT ALSO HUMAN BEINGS.
TOOLS OF VARYING DEGREES OF USEFULNESS HAVE BEEN PUT IN PLACE TO SAVE THEM AND MANAGE FISHING.
ALL THIS HAS BEEN MADE POSSIBLE BY MAJOR ADVANCES IN OUR KNOWLEDGE ABOUT SHARKS OVER THE LAST FEW DECADES.
RECENT PROGRESS HAS OPENED UP SEVERAL FIELDS OF RESEARCH.
NEW MATHEMATICAL MODELS ALLOWING ECOSYSTEMIC MANAGEMENT OF HALIEUTIC* RESOURCES, INCLUDING SHARKS, MUST BE PERFECTED IN THE NEAR FUTURE.

*HAVING TO DO WITH THE ART OR PRACTICE OF FISHING AND LIVING MARINE RESOURCES

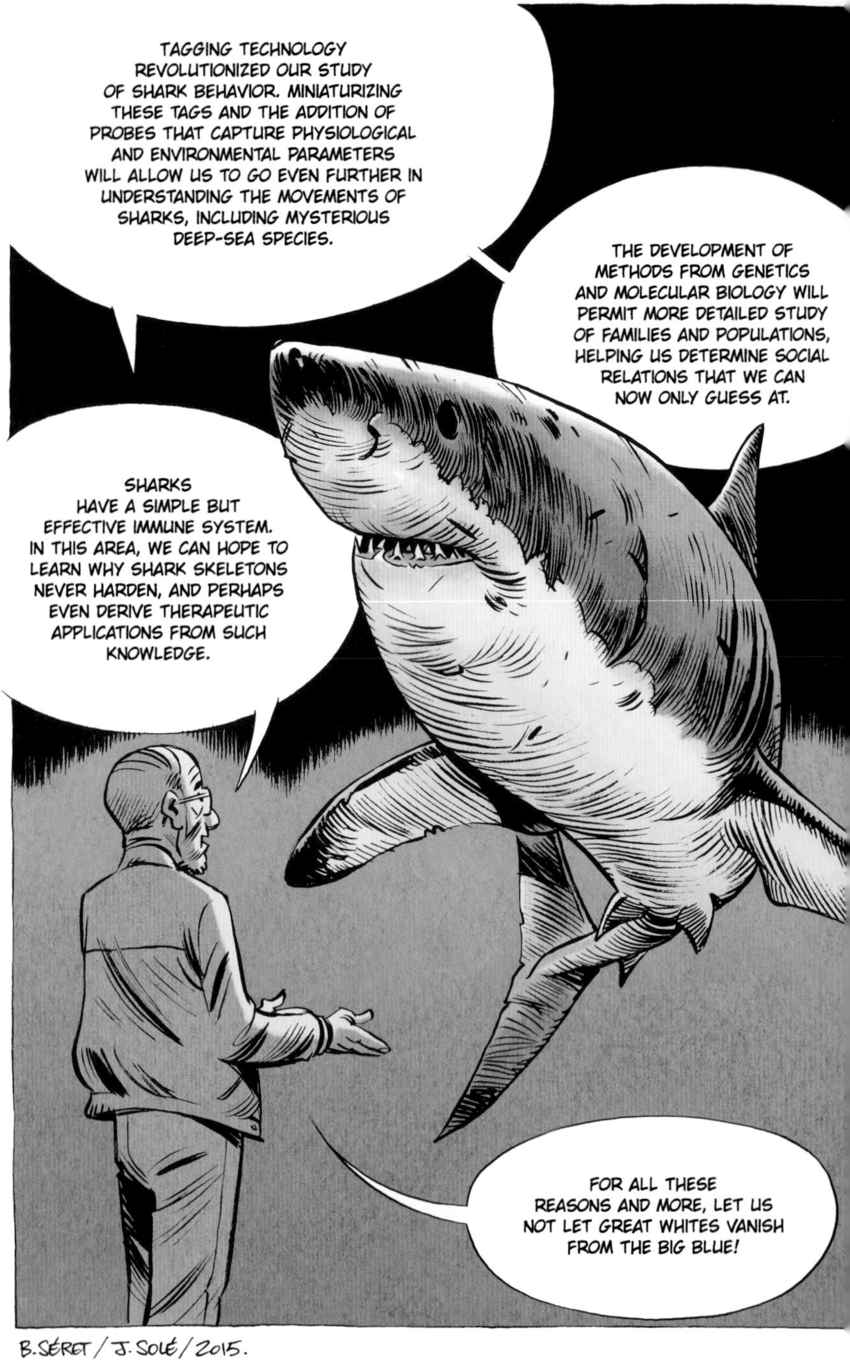
TAGGING TECHNOLOGY REVOLUTIONIZED OUR STUDY OF SHARK BEHAVIOR. MINIATURIZING THESE TAGS AND THE ADDITION OF PROBES THAT CAPTURE PHYSIOLOGICAL AND ENVIRONMENTAL PARAMETERS WILL ALLOW US TO GO EVEN FURTHER IN UNDERSTANDING THE MOVEMENTS OF SHARKS, INCLUDING MYSTERIOUS DEEP-SEA SPECIES.
THE DEVELOPMENT OF METHODS FROM GENETICS AND MOLECULAR BIOLOGY WILL PERMIT MORE DETAILED STUDY OF FAMILIES AND POPULATIONS, HELPING US DETERMINE SOCIAL RELATIONS THAT WE CAN NOW ONLY GUESS AT.
SHARKS HAVE A SIMPLE BUT EFFECTIVE IMMUNE SYSTEM. IN THIS AREA, WE CAN HOPE TO LEARN WHY SHARK SKELETONS NEVER HARDEN, AND PERHAPS EVEN DERIVE THERAPEUTIC APPLICATIONS FROM SUCH KNOWLEDGE.
FOR ALL THESE REASONS AND MORE, LET US NOT LET GREAT WHITES VANISH FROM THE BIG BLUE!

B. SÉRET / J. SOLÉ / 2015.

TO LEARN MORE

THREE SUGGESTIONS BY BERNARD SÉRET

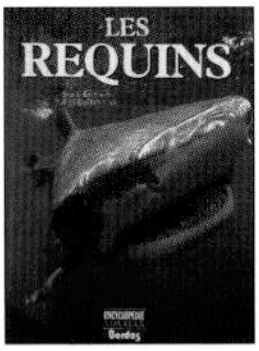
LES
REQUINS

The Sharks, edited by John D. Stevens, collected works, Facts on File, 1987. Despite being more than 30 years old, this popular Australian work remains one of the best. The chapters were all written by renowned "sharkologists!"

Requin: de la prehistoire a nos jours (Sharks: From Prehistory to Today). Book by Gilles Cuny and Alain Benetau, coll. "Bilbiotheque scientifique" ("part of the "Scientific Library" collection), Belin, 2013. A superb dive into the history of sharks accompanied by magnificent illustrations. A passionate journey through time in the company of the strange creatures sharks came from.

Not published in English

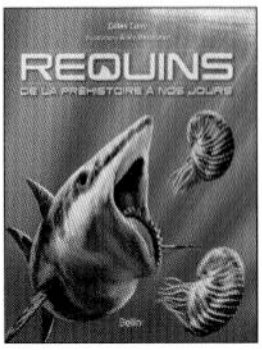
REQUINS

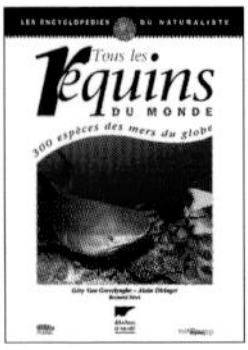
Tous les
Requins
DU MONDE

Tous les requins du monde. 300 espesces des mers du globe (All the sharks in the world: 300 species from the planet's oceans) book by Géry Van Grevelynghe, Bernard Séret and Alain Diringer, coll. "Les encyclopédies du naturaliste." (part of the "Naturalist Ecyclopedia" collection), Delachaux & Niestlé, 1999. A selection of 300 species for sharks to learn to tell them apart.

Not published in English

THREE SUGGESTIONS BY JULIEN SOLÉ

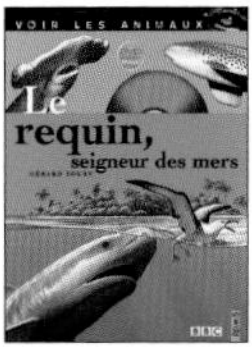
VOIR LES ANIMAUX
Le requin,
seigneur des mers
BBC

Le requin, **seigneur des mers (Sharks, lord of the seas), book by Gérard Soury, Fleurus, 2007.** This work meant first and foremost for young readers covers the anatomy, reproduction, and hunting methods of the most famous sharks. The book is accompanied by a DVD produced by the BBC, *La guerre des requins (The Shark War)*, a 52 minute documentary that shows some rare scenes like, for example, the birth of a lemon shark.

Not published in English

Shark Book, **book by Julien Solé, Fluide Glacial, 2014.** My passion for sharks came from my five year old son and, ever since, I haven't been able to stop drawing them. *Shark Book*, published as a sketchbook, contains more than 200 sharks, some imaginary, wacky funny, and scientifically incorrect!

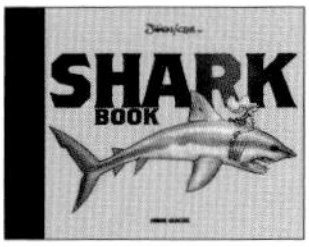
SHARK
BOOK

Not published in English

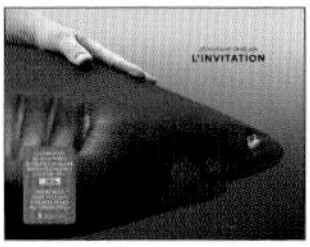
L'INVITATION

Shark: Fear and Beauty, **book by Jean-Marie Ghislain, Thames & Hudson, 2014.** In order to overcome his phobia of sharks, Jean-Marie Ghislain decided to dive to meet them with his camera in order to learn to love and respect them. This black and white album of photographs, with pictures taken from the perspective of the human eye, communicates the emotion that a shark encounter can bring and displays them in their natural habitants. There are no malformed little sharks here like those Bernard Séret likes, but rather, a selection of sharks as if out of a beauty contest, built like warheads.

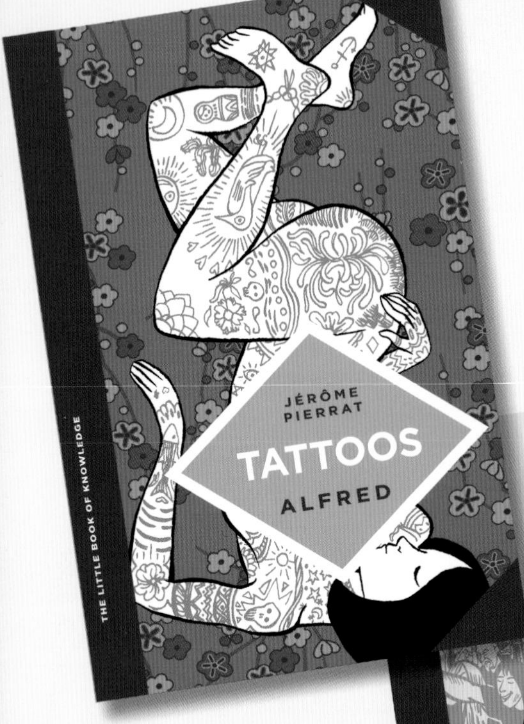
THE LITTLE BOOK OF KNOWLEDGE
JÉRÔME
PIERRAT
TATTOOS
ALFRED

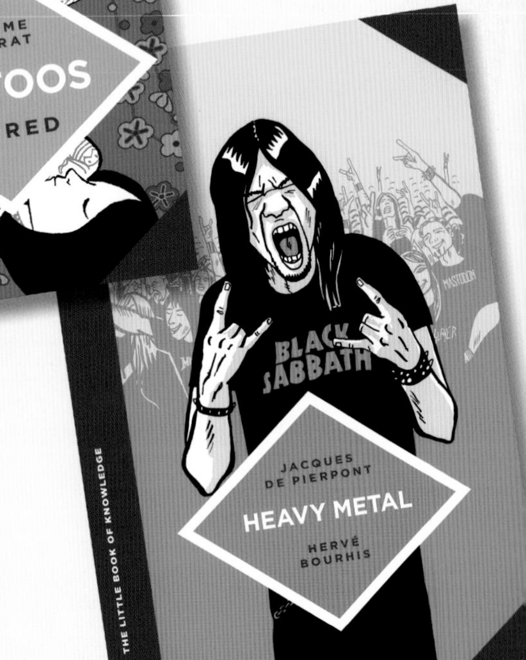
THE LITTLE BOOK OF KNOWLEDGE
BLACK
SABBATH
JACQUES
DE PIERPONT
HEAVY METAL
HERVÉ
BOURHIS

HESE *LITTLE BOOKS OF KNOWLEDGE*

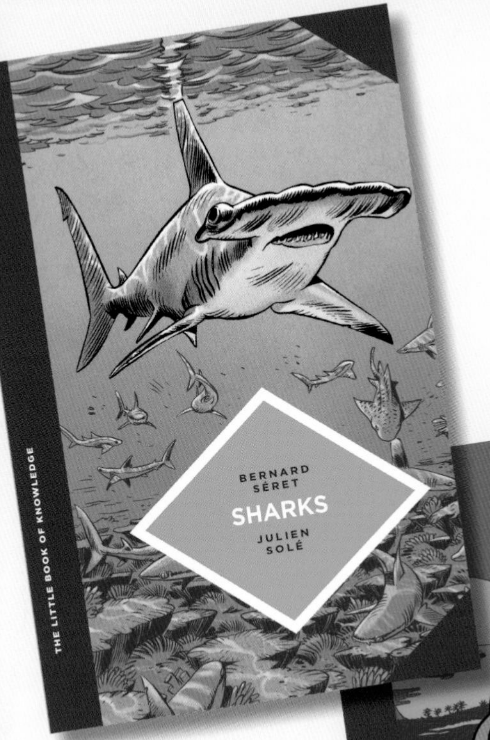
THE LITTLE BOOK OF KNOWLEDGE
BERNARD SÉRET
SHARKS
JULIEN SOLÉ

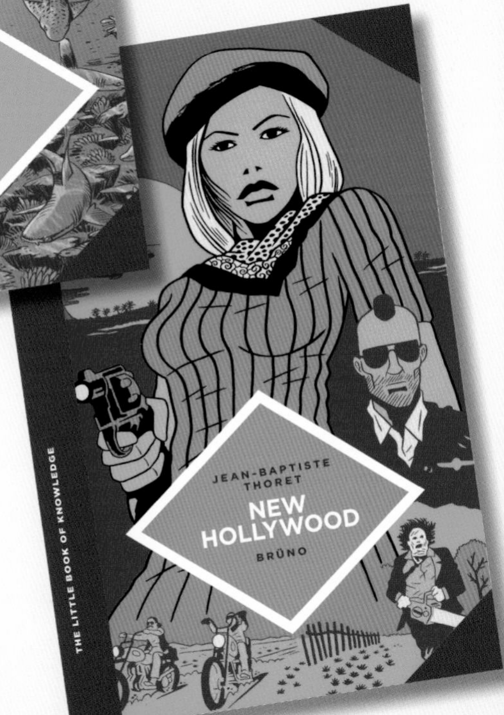
THE LITTLE BOOK OF KNOWLEDGE
JEAN-BAPTISTE THORET
NEW HOLLYWOOD
BRÜNO

THE LITTLE BOOK
OF KNOWLEDGE:

SHARKS